GramGram Plus 3

Author Hyunjeong, Kim **Consultant** Prof. Eunyoung, Park **Editorial Supervisor** LLS English Research Center

J PLUS
Language Publishing Co.

Have Fun and Enjoy
the
GRAM GRAM PLUS Series

Welcome to the GRAM GRAM PLUS Series.

This is an introductory grammar series designed to be fun and easy for young learners. It is also designed to promote accurate English speaking and writing skills.

Korean students have traditionally learned English grammar through rote memorization. However, I believe that grammar learning is more effectively realized when instruction is paired with practice. With clear explanations, imaginative illustrations, enjoyable grammar activities and games, the GRAM GRAM PLUS Series allows students to enjoy English grammar as they learn how to use it properly.

The GRAM GRAM PLUS Series provides students with ample opportunities to both practice and improve their English.

Author: Hyunjeong, Kim

Supervisor's Recommendation

Traditionally, many language teachers have taught English grammar according to the Grammar Translation Method. In grammar-translation classes, students learn grammatical rules and then apply those rules by translating sentences between the target language and their native language. Advanced students may be required to translate whole texts word-for-word. However, at the height of the Communicative Approach to language learning in the 1980s and early 1990s, it became fashionable in some quarters to deride so-called "old-fashioned" methods and, in particular, something broadly labeled "Grammar Translation". Nevertheless, we can't ignore grammar in language teaching and learning. In that sense, this series can help both teachers and students by presenting grammar in a communicative way, which can be a very fascinating way to learn English grammar. With a lot of pictures, cartoons, games, and activities, children will be able to 'acquire' English grammar, not to 'study' grammar. I hope that many kids will enjoy this joyful process!

Consultant: Prof. Eunyoung, Park

(Ph. D. in English Education / Professor at Methodist Theological University)

GRAM GRAM PLUS BOOK 3

Unit	Title		Grammar	Topic/Theme	Vocabulary	문법포인트
1	Can You Play Soccer?	Helping Verb	- Ability: Auxiliary "Can" can / can't	Sports	- play soccer, play tennis, play basketball, play volleyball, play baseball, play badminton	
2	You Should Wear A Helmet		- Obligation: Auxiliary "Should" should / shouldn't	Leisure	- wear a helmet, be late, take off shoes, wear knee pads, be quiet, play computer games	
3	You Must Speak In English		- Subjective Obligation "Must" must / must not	School Rules	- be late, litter, run, make noise, fight, cheat	
4	You Have To Be On Time		- Objective Obligation: "Have To" have to / don't have to	Manners	- be on time, wait one's turn, ask to pass the salt, give up one's seat, cover one's mouth	
5	The Party Was Great!	Past Simple	- Past Simple Tense: "Be" Verbs was / wasn't / were / weren't	Holidays	- Christmas, Thanksgiving, New Year's Day, Halloween, Valentine's Day, Children's Day	
6	My Family Watched A Movie		- Past Simple Tense: "General Verbs" 1 Regular Past Form: watched / played / invited	Family Events	- watch, play badminton, invite, climb, enjoy, visit	
7	We Took A Trip		- Past Simple Tense: "General Verbs" 2 Irregular Past Form: went / took / forgot	Trips	- take a picture, eat seafood, go shopping, buy a gift, swim at the beach, write a postcard	
8	Did You Have A Good Time?		- Past Simple Tense: Questions Did ~ ? / What did ~?	School Field Trips	- zoo, fire station, museum, TV station, aquarium, amusement park	

Unit	Title		Grammar	Topic/Theme	Vocabulary	문법포인트
9	I Am Making Cookies	Present & Past Continuous	- Present Continuous: Be Verbs + ~ing am(are/is) + ~ing / am(are/is) + not + ~ing	Hobbies	- swim, cook, draw a picture, collect shells, take a photo, play the piano	
10	I Was Doing My Homework		- Past Continuous: Be Verbs + ~ing was(were) + ~ing / was+ not + ~ing	After School Activities	- do homework, learn Taekwondo, take a walk, read a book, ride a bike, take a piano lesson	
11	Are You Cleaning Your Room?		- Question Continuous: Be Verbs Am(Are/Is) + ~ing?	House Chores	- set the table, clean the room, water the plants, do the dishes, vacuum the floor, take out the trash	
12	What Was He Doing?		- WH-Questions: "What / Where"	School Clubs	- sing in chorus, interview, play music, see the stars, exercise, watch a movie	
13	It Is Under The Desk	Prepositions & There is/are ~	- Prepositions Of Places 1: in / on / under / in front of / behind	In My Room	- on the wall, behind the desk, under the chair, in the closet, in front of the computer	
14	It Is Next To The Hospital		- Prepositions Of Places 2: next to / between / across from	Buildings	- post office, hospital, movie theater, police station, bank, fire station	
15	There Is A Zoo In My Town		- There + Be Verbs	Places In The Town	- museum, concert hall, fish market, train station, old palace, library	
16	Where Is The Bakery?		- WH-Questions: "Where"	Stores	- bakery, clothing store, ice cream shop, bookstore, supermakret, stationery store	

일러두기

GRAM'S TALK

해당 유닛의 핵심 주제와 관련된 단어와 어구를 하나의 재미있는 상황으로 설정하여 삽화로 제시하였습니다. 한눈에 보이는 그림을 통해 핵심 단어들을 쉽고 빠르게 파악할 수 있습니다.

GRAM'S Expressions

해당 유닛의 주제와 연관된 핵심 단어, 어구를 제시하였습니다. 단어를 듣고 알맞은 그림을 찾는활동을 하며, 주제 중심 핵심 단어들을 체크해 봅니다.

Hello!
I'm Gram!

Easy to Follow

6 STEP
Lesson Process

STEP 2

GRAM POINT

해당 유닛의 문법 포인트를 간단한 설명과 도표로 제시하였습니다. 문법 체계에 대한 분석 없이 하나의 문법 사항을 하나의 도표로 빠르게 학습할 수 있습니다. 친절한 GRAM의 한국말 설명은 문법 포인트에 대한 빠른 이해를 도와줍니다.

GRAM CHECK-UP

위에서 확인한 문법 포인트를 간단한 확인문제를 통해 확인해 볼 수 있습니다.

STEP 3

GRAM PRACTICE

해당 유닛의 주제 중심 단어와 문법 포인트를 확인할 수 있는 다양한 형식의 액티비티를 제시하였습니다. 빈칸 채우기, 알맞은 말 고르기, 표 보고 문장 완성하기, 잘못된 표현 고치기 등의 다양한 형식의 액티비티를 통해 앞서 익힌 단어와 문법 포인트를 쉽고 재미있게 정리해 볼 수 있습니다.

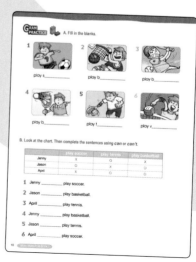

STEP 6

FUNNY GRAM

해당 유닛의 문법 포인트와 핵심 단어를 활용한 게임을 제시하였습니다.
다양한 유형의 게임을 통해 해당 유닛의 문법 포인트와 핵심 단어를 마지막으로 정리, 확인할 수 있도록 하였습니다.

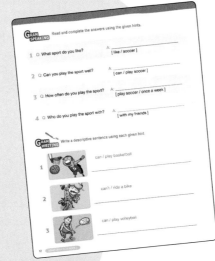

STEP 5

GRAM SPEAKING

그림보고 질문에 답하기/연계질문에 답하기/그림묘사하기/문제 해결하기 등 'Speaking Activity'를 제시하였습니다.

GRAM WRITING

그림 선택해서 묘사하기/그림 세부 묘사하기/편지쓰기/추론하여 글쓰기 등의 'Writing Activity'를 제시하였습니다. 앞서 익힌 '문법'을 실제로 '활용'할 수 있는 기회를 통해 실용적인 문법 학습은 물론, 각종 시험에 대한 대비도 할 수 있습니다

STEP 4

GRAM READING

해당 유닛의 문법 포인트가 포함된 80자 이내의 리딩 지문을 제시하였습니다. 익숙하고도 재미있는 상황으로 구성된 리딩 지문을 읽으며 문법이 실제 활용되는 예를 자연스럽게 확인할 수 있습니다.

GRAM Comprehension

읽은 내용을 확인해 볼 수 있는 주관식 문제를 제시하였습니다. 해당 유닛의 문법 포인트를 활용할 수 있도록 하였습니다.

Unit 01

Can You Play Soccer?

  GRAM TALK Track 1 ☐ Listen ☐ Repeat ☐ Role play

Can you play soccer?

Yes, I can.

I can kick the ball.

KICK!

I can pass the ball, too.

PASS!

GOAL!

Can you score a goal, too?

Oh, my!

No, I can't.

 **GRAM Expressions** Track 2 ABC Listen and number the pictures in order. Track 3

play soccer

play tennis

play basketball

play volleyball

play baseball

play badminton

GRAM POINT Can / Can't / Can you~?

- We use can + verb to talk about ability.
- We use cannot + verb to talk about inability.

	Positive	Negative
I / You He / She / It We / You / They	can swim.	can't swim.

- We put can before the subject to make a question.

Can	I / you he / she / it we / you / they	swim?

Ex   Q: Can you swim?

A: Yes, I can. / No, I can't.

'~을 할 수 있다'는 'can'을
사용하고, '~을 할 수 없다'는
'can't'를 사용해!

GRAM CHECK UP   Look and write *can* or *can't*.

1

He _____ skate.

2

He _____ play baseball.

3

He _____ skate.

4

She _____ play baseball.

 **A. Fill in the blanks.**

1

play s_____

2

play b_____

3

play b_____

4

play b_____

5

play t_____

6

play v_____

B. Look at the chart. Then complete the sentences using _can_ or _can't_.

	play soccer	play tennis	play basketball
Jenny	X	O	X
Jason	O	X	O
April	X	O	O

1 Jenny _____ play soccer.

2 Jason _____ play basketball.

3 April _____ play tennis.

4 Jenny _____ play basketball.

5 Jason _____ play tennis.

6 April _____ play soccer.

I Like Sports!

My name is Jason. I really like sports.
I can play basketball.
I play basketball three times a week.
I can play basketball at the gym.

When I play basketball,
I can pass the ball.
I can bounce the ball, too.
But, I can't shoot the ball well.
So, I can't score points.
I'm going to practice every day.

> gym 체육관   bounce 공을 튀기다   shoot 슛을 던지다   score 득점을 하다   practice 연습하다   be going to ~를 할 것이다

GRAM COMPREHENSION

1 Can Jason pass the ball?

_____

2 Can Jason bounce the ball?

_____

3 Can Jason shoot the ball well?

_____

Read and complete the answers using the given hints.

1 Q: What sport do you like?   A: _____

[like / soccer]

2 Q: Can you play the sport well?   A: _____

[can / play soccer]

3 Q: How often do you play the sport?   A: _____

[play soccer / once a week]

4 Q: Who do you play the sport with?   A: _____

[with my friends]

GRAM WRITING   **Write a descriptive sentence using each given hint.**

1    can / play basketball

_____

2    can't / ride a bike

_____

3    can / play volleyball

_____

FUNNY GRAM

Rabbit & Turtle Race

Fill the circles with verbs you are working on in the unit.

Prepare the CAN or CAN'T die and the game markers.

When it's your turn, roll the die and say a sentence like *"I can (can't) play tennis."* If you can play the sport, you get to stay on the space. If you can't, you have to go back.

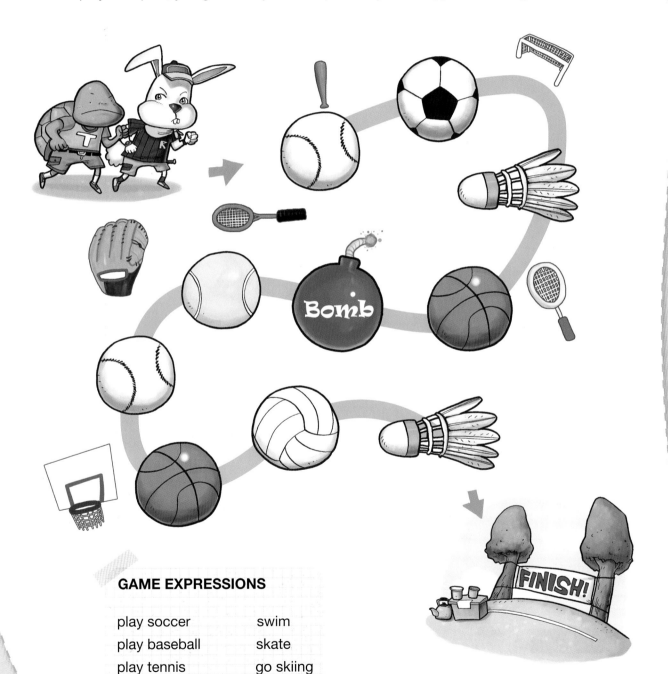

GAME EXPRESSIONS

play soccer	swim
play baseball	skate
play tennis	go skiing
play basketball	

Unit 02 You Should Wear A Helmet

GRAM TALK
Track 5 □ Listen □ Repeat □ Role play

Let's in-line skate tomorrow.

Good idea!

Should I wear a helmet?

Yes, you should.

Should I wear knee pads, too?

Yes, you should.

Anything else?

You shouldn't be late.

OK.

GRAM Expressions
Track 6 ABC Listen and number the pictures in order. Track 7

wear a helmet

be late

take off shoes

wear knee pads

be quiet

play computer games

GRAM POINT — Should / Should Not / Should I ~?

- We use should + verb to express advice. It means that something is a good idea.
- We use should not + verb to say that something isn't a good idea.

	Positive	Negative	
I / You		should not wear (=shouldn't)	
He / She / It	should wear		a hat.
We / You / They			

- We put should before the subject to make a question.

Ex Q: Should I wear a hat?

A: Yes, you should. / No, you shouldn't.

'~하는 게 좋다' 또는 '~해야 한다'라는 뜻의 권유나 충고를 나타낼 때는 'should'를 사용하고, '~하지 않는 게 좋겠다'라고 말할 때는 'shouldn't'를 사용해.

 **Look and write should or shouldn't.**

1

You _____ be late.

2

You _____ stretch first.

3

You _____ wear knee pads.

4

You _____ play computer games.

 **A. Use words from the box to fill in the blanks.**

Word Box	knee pads late play wear quiet take off

1

_____ shoes

2

be _____

3

_____ a helmet

4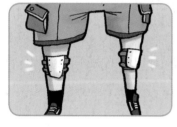

wear _____

5

be _____

6

_____ computer games

B. Rewrite the sentences using _should_ or _shouldn't_.

> Eric brings hiking boots. [should] → Eric should bring hiking boots.

1 Ryan brings knee pads. [shouldn't]

_____

2 Angela brings a helmet. [should]

_____

3 Brian brings a swimming hat. [shouldn't]

_____

02

Let's Go Camping

Dear Alice,

My family will go hiking up the mountain.

Let's go together.

You should bring your hiking boots.

You should bring a hat and warm clothes, too.

My mother will cook, so you shouldn't bring a lunch.

You should come to my house by nine o'clock on Saturday.

You shouldn't be late.

See you on Saturday.

Cindy

mountain 산   hiking boots 등산화   warm 따뜻한   cook 요리하다   prepare 준비하다

GRAM **COMPREHENSION**

1 Should Alice bring her hiking boots?

_____

2 Should Alice bring a lunch?

_____

3 Should Alice come to Cindy's house on Saturday?

_____

GRAM **SPEAKING**   Read and complete the answers using the given hints.

1   Q: Your friend asks you to ride a bike today, but you can't. You should go hiking with your father. What would you say to your friend?

A: I'm sorry, but I can't. _____

should / with my father / go hiking

2   Q: Your friend asks you to go swimming today, but you can't. You should go to the movies with Julie. What would you say to your friend?

A: I'm sorry, but I can't. _____

should / go to the movies / with Julie

 **G**RAM **WRITING**   Look and complete the sentences using the given hints.

shouldn't be late / should wear a helmet and knee pads / should go to my room and bring them

1   Ted is going to snowboarding camp. His friend looks at him and says,

"You _____."

2   "Oh, I forgot," he answers.

"I _____."

3   She looks at her watch and says to him,

"You _____."

Funny Gram

Bingo Game!

Cut out the picture cards and put them on any of the spaces on the board.
Say the sentences in turns.
Ex O → You should wear a helmet.
    X → You shouldn't be late.
If you say the sentence correctly, turn over the card.
When you make two lines, you say "BINGO!"

△ wear a helmet
△ be late
△ take off your shoes
△ go camping
△ go to the movies
△ wear knee pads

△ be quiet
△ wear a swimming cap
△ prepare the lunch
△ play computer games
△ in-line skate

You Must Speak In English

GRAM TALK Track 9 □ Listen □ Repeat □ Role play

GRAM Expressions Track 10 ABC Listen and number the pictures in order. Track 11

be late   litter   run   be noisy   fight   cheat

GRAM POINT Must / Mustn't

- We use must + verb to express duty or necessity. It means that something is necessary.

- We use must not + verb to express prohibition. It means "Don't do something."

	Positive	Negative	
I / You			
He / She	must speak	must not speak (mustn't)	in Korean.
We / You / They			

Ex You must be quiet in the library.

You must not (mustn't) be noisy in the library.

'~해야 한다'는 뜻의 의무나 필요를 나타낼 때는 'must'를 사용하고, '~해서는 안 된다'는 뜻의 강한 금지를 나타낼 때는 'mustn't'를 사용하자.

GRAM CHECK UP

Look and write *must* or *mustn't*.

1

He _____ speak in Korean.

2

She _____ be quiet in class.

3

He _____ speak in English.

4

She _____ be noisy in class.

 **A. Fill in the blanks.**

1

r_____ in the hallway

2

be n_____

3

be l_____

4

c_____ in the exam

5

l_____

6

f_____ with classmates

B. Check each expression G(good) or B(bad). Then complete the sentences using
***must* or *must not*.**

1. run in the hallway	G	B	4. fight with classmates	G	B
2. litter in school	G	B	5. cheat in the exam	G	B
3. follow the school rules	G	B	6. use a cellphone in class	G	B

1 You _____ run in the hallway.

2 You _____ litter in school.

3 You _____ follow the school rules.

4 You _____ fight with classmates.

5 You _____ cheat in the exam.

6 You _____ use a cell phone in class.

GRAM **READING** Read and answer the questions.

Please Follow The School Rules

Good morning, students.
I'm Mr. Henson.
I will tell you three school rules.
You must follow them.
First, you must not make fun of
your classmates.
Second, you must not talk loudly
in the library.
You must be quiet there.
Third, you must not litter in school.
You must put trash in the trash can.
Please follow the rules.

follow 따르다   make fun of ~를 놀리다   loudly 크게   library 도서관   trash 쓰레기   litter 어지럽히다

GRAM **COMPREHENSION** Correct the sentences according to the story above.

1 Students must make fun of their classmates.

_____

2 Students must not be quiet in the library.

_____

3 Students must litter in school.

_____

G RAM SPEAKING

Look and number the sentences in order.
Then, fill in the blanks with *must* or *must not*.

1  2  3  4  5

[ ] She answers, "OK. See you tomorrow."

[1] A new girl comes to class.

[ ] In the library, he says to her, "You _____ be noisy here."

[ ] A boy tells her, " _____ run in the hall way."

[ ] On the way home, he tells her, "You _____ be late for school."

G RAM WRITING

 Write what each person *must not* do using the given expressions.

Maggie   Susie   Nick

1 Susie _____.
   [litter]

2 Nick _____.
   [use a cellphone at school]

3 Maggie _____.
   [run in the classroom]

Cut out the cards and complete the sentences for the pictures using *must* or *must not*.
Then, make your own mini-book.

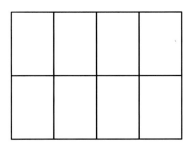

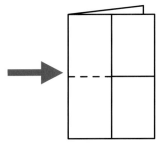

Fold paper on all lines, and open up

Fold paper in half, and cut along the dotted line.

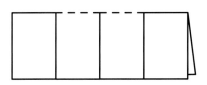

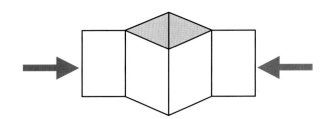

Open and fold like above.

Push in on both ends.

Fold the book.

You Have To Be On Time

  Listen □ **Repeat** □ **Role play**

GRAM Expressions ABC Listen and number the pictures in order.

be on time

wait one's turn

ask to pass the salt

give up one's seat

cover one's mouth

GRAM POINT — Have To / Don't Have To / Do I Have To ~?

- We use have (has) to + verb to express necessity. It means that something is necessary.

  We use don't (doesn't) have to + verb to say that something is not necessary.

	Positive	Negative	
I / You	have to use	don't have to use	a spoon.
We / You / They			
He / She	has to use	doesn't have to use	

- We put Do (Does) before the subject to make a question.

Ex Q: Do I have to use a spoon?

A: Yes, you have to. / No, you don't have to.

'~할 필요가 있다' 또는 '~해야 한다'고 말할 때는 'have(has) to'를 사용하고, '~할 필요가 없다'고 말할 때는 'don't(doesn't) have to'를 사용하자.

GRAM CHECK UP

Look and write **have to**, **has to**, **don't have to**, or **doesn't have to**.

1

I _____ wear a dress.

2

He _____ take off his shoes.

3

I _____ wear a dress.

4

He _____ take off his shoes.

1

wait one's t_____

2

be on t_____

3

ask to p_____ the salt

4

g_____ up one's seat

5

c_____ one's mouth

B. Correct the mistakes in the following sentences.

1 He have to give up his seat.

_____.

2 I have lots of time. I don't has to hurry.

_____.

3 We doesn't have to wait our turn.

_____.

4 I has to cover my mouth when coughing.

_____.

5 You has to chew with your mouth closed.

_____.

6 She don't have to wear a dress to the party.

_____.

Read and answer the questions.

Enjoy The Movie!

Attention, students.
I have tickets for you, so you
don't have to buy tickets.
When you get a ticket, you have to
check your seat numbers.
Before the movie starts, you have to
turn off your cell phones.
You have to talk quietly during
the movie.
Please don't be noisy.
Enjoy the movie.

enjoy 즐기다   attention 주목, 집중   ticket 입장권, 표   check 확인하다   seat 좌석   soon 곧   during ~동안

GRAM COMPREHENSION

1 Do the students have to buy their tickets?

_____

2 Do the students have to check their seat numbers?

_____

3 Do the students have to turn off their cellphones?

_____

 **RAM SPEAKING** Look and answer the questions using the given hints.

1  Does the girl have to give up her seat?

_____

has to / give up

2 Do they have to talk loudly?

_____

have to / be quiet

3 Does the girl have to turn off her camera?

_____

has to / turn off

 **RAM WRITING** Write an email telling your friend about manners in a concert using the given expressions.

Hi Kelly,

I want to talk to you about using manners in a concert.

First, you _____ _____. Don't be late.

Second, you _____ _____ before the concert.

Third, you _____ _____ during the concert.

Enjoy the concert.

Minji

have to   be on time   turn off one's cell phone   be quiet

FUNNY GRAM

Spinner

Use a pencil and a paper clip. Prepare the HAVE TO or DON'T HAVE TO die. During your turn, spin the paper clip and roll the die. Then, say a sentence like *"You have to (don't have to) wear a dress."*

The Party Was Great!

 GRAM TALK Track 17 ☐ Listen ☐ Repeat ☐ Role play

How was your Christmas?

It was great!

Were you at home?

No, I wasn't.

I was at Jason's Christmas party.

The Christmas music was good.

The food was delicious, too.

GRAM Expressions Track 18 Listen and number the pictures in order. Track 19

Christmas

Thanksgiving

New Year's Day

Halloween

Valentine's Day

Children's Day

GRAM POINT — Was / Were

- We use the simple past to express the past.

  Was is the simple past of am and is.

  Were is the simple past of are.

	Positive	Negative	
I He / She / It	was	was not (wasn't)	late.
We / You / They	were	were not (weren't)	

- We put was or were before the subject to make a question.

  Ex Q: Were you happy with the present?

  A: Yes, I was. / No, I wasn't.

> be동사의 과거형은 두 가지가 있어.
> 주어가 1인칭 단수일 때와 3인칭 단수
> 일 때는 'was'를, 2인칭이나
> 복수일 때는 'were'를 사용한다는
> 것을 기억하자!

GRAM CHECK UP

Look and write **was** or **were**.

1 The turkey _____ very delicious.

2 I _____ excited about the sunrise.

3 _____ the Christmas parade interesting?

4 _____ your parents happy with the chocolates?

 **A. Match the pictures with the correct holidays and words.**

1	2	3	4	5

Christmas   Valentine's Day   Thanksgiving   Halloween   New Year's Day

costume   sunrise   chocolate   turkey   gingerbread

B. Choose the correct forms.

1 Amy's Halloween costume | is / was | funny last year.

2 I | was / wasn't | at Sam's Christmas party. I was sick.

3 We | are / was / were | excited with the party yesterday.

4 The costume contest | was / were | so much fun.

5 The turkey | was / wasn't | delicious. It was terrible.

6 Last year the Christmas parade | is / are / was / were | interesting.

7 Going trick-or-treating | is / are / was / were | really exciting last night.

How Was Your Halloween?

Last Thursday was Halloween.
My sister and I were at Ben's Halloween party.
The party was so much fun.
The food was delicious.
We had a Halloween costume contest there.
My rabbit costume was good, but I wasn't the winner.
The winner was Susie.
Her pumpkin costume was so cute.

fun 재미   contest 대회, 경연   costume 의상   winner 우승자   delicious 맛있는

GRAM COMPREHENSION

1 Was the girl at home on Halloween?

_____

2 Was the party so much fun?

_____

3 Was Susie's costume cute?

_____

GRAM **SPEAKING** Look and answer the questions using the given hints.

1

Where was the boy?

_____

at the Christmas party

2

Was the girl happy?

_____

sad

3

Were the boy and the girl hungry?

_____

full

GRAM **WRITING** Look and complete the sentences using the given hints.

wasn't big

was excited

weren't happy

were in the living room

It was Christmas morning.

1 The boy and his family _____.

2 The Christmas tree _____.

3 The boy _____ with the presents.

4 The girls _____ with the sweaters.

Toss The Coin

Toss the coin on the table. Move 1 space for heads and 2 spaces for tails. Then, change the sentences into their past forms.

(For example, It *is* delicious. → It *was* delicious.)

START

| The food *is* delicious. | → | The party *isn't* fun. | → | I *am* excited. | → | They *are* happy. |

| She *isn't* there. | ← | He *is* in the room. | ← | They *are* happy. | ← | The game *is* exciting. |

| You *are* surprised. | → | It *isn't* fun. | → | The costume *is* good. | → | They *are* excited. |

| They *aren't* surprised. | ← | It *isn't* fun. | ← | The trip *is* exciting. | ← | The game *is* fun. |

FINISH

My Family Watched A Movie

 GRAM TALK Track 21 □ Listen □ Repeat □ Role play

How was your weekend? Great.

My family watched a movie.

Then we visited our grandparents.

We talked about our trip to Busan.

We arrived home very late.

I was so tired.

 **GRAM Expressions** Track 22 ABC Listen and number the pictures in order. Track 23

 watch
 play badminton
 invite
 climb
 enjoy
 visit

GRAM POINT — Watched / Studied / Invited

- We use the simple past to talk about activities or situations in the past.
  We should use did not + verb in negative.

	Positive	Negative	
I / He / She / It We / You / They	watched	did not watch (didn't)	a movie yesterday.

- We usually add – ed to a verb to form the simple past.

– ed	watch – watch**ed** visit – visit**ed** order – order**ed** plan – plann**ed**	play – play**ed** cook – cook**ed** wait – wait**ed** stop – stop**ped**
(–e) + – d	like – lik**ed** invite – invit**ed**	arrive – arriv**ed** dance – danc**ed**
(-y) → i + – ed	study – stud**ied**	try – tr**ied**

06

동사의 과거형은 보통 동사원형 뒤에 '–ed'를 붙이는데, '–e'로 끝날 때는 '–d'만 붙이고, '자음+–y'로 끝날 때는 y를 i로 바꾸고 '–ed'를 붙여야 해! 그리고! '단모음+단자음'으로 끝날 때는 자음을 한 번 더 쓰고 '–ed'를 붙이는 것도 기억하자!

GRAM CHECK UP

Complete the sentences to use the past tense.

1 My family _____ the museum yesterday. [visit]

2 We _____ badminton last Sunday. [play]

3 We _____ pasta for dinner last night. [cook]

4 My family _____ a movie last weekend. [watch]

 **A. Fill in the blanks.**

1

i_____ friends

2

c_____ a mountain

3

v_____ a museum

4

e_____ the birthday party

5

p_____ badminton

6

w_____ a movie

B. Change the sentences into the past forms.

1 My sister likes her birthday presents.

_____.

2 We don't invite our friends to the party.

_____.

3 My parents plan a trip to Paris.

_____.

4 I don't wait for my brother at the station.

_____.

5 We enjoy my brother's birthday.

_____.

Surprise Party For Mom!

My name is Brian.
Last Saturday was my mom's birthday.
My dad and I planned a surprise
party for her.
We prepared many balloons.
We invited my mom's friends to
the party.
We cooked her favorite food, too.
We turned off the lights and waited
for her.
We shouted, "Happy Birthday!"
She really liked the party.

surprise party 깜짝 파티	prepare 준비하다	balloon 풍선	favorite 가장 좋아하는
turn off (불을) 끄다	shout 큰 소리로 말하다	wait for ~를 기다리다	

GRAM **COMPREHENSION**

1 What did Brian plan for his mom?

_____

2 What did Brian's family prepare?

_____

3 Who did Brian invite?

_____

GRAM SPEAKING Read and complete the answers using the given hints.

1 Q: How was your birthday last year? [great]

A: _____

2 Q: Did your family celebrate your birthday? [enjoy / my birthday]

A: _____

3 Q: Did your mom cook delicious food? [cook / delicious food]

A: _____

4 Q: Did you invite your friends? [invite / my friends]

A: _____

GRAM WRITING Write a descriptive sentence using the given hints.

1  climb a mountain / last weekend

_____

2  enjoy my birthday / yesterday

_____

3  visit a museum / last Saturday

_____

Word Search

Find and circle the past forms of the given words.

For example, *watch* → *watched*

☑ watch   ☐ play

☐ order   ☐ visit

☐ plan   ☐ like

☐ dance   ☐ arrive

☐ study   ☐ try

V	T	R	I	E	D	C	O	Q	S
I	S	A	P	W	T	N	R	A	T
S	W	P	L	A	Y	E	D	R	U
I	B	E	A	T	E	N	E	R	D
T	D	A	N	C	E	D	R	I	I
E	A	T	E	H	R	A	E	V	E
D	N	O	D	E	S	R	D	E	D
L	I	K	E	D	M	S	O	D	D

Unit 07
We Took A Trip

  GRAM TALK (Track 25) ☐ Listen ☐ Repeat ☐ Role play

Did you go to Jeju?

Yes. My family took a trip.

Did you have a good time?

Yes, we did.

We swam at the beach.

Yes, we did.

Did you eat seafood?

It was delicious!

Good!

 **GRAM Expressions** (Track 26) **ABC** Listen and number the pictures in order. (Track 27)

take a picture

eat seafood

go shopping

buy a gift

swim at the beach

write a postcard

GRAM POINT — Went, Ate, Swam

- We use the simple past to talk about activities or situations in the past. We should use did not + verb for the negative form.

	Positive	Negative	
I / He / She / It We / You / They	went	did not go (didn't)	to Busan last weekend.

- Some verbs are irregular. The simple past is not – ed.

go – went	come – came	have – had
get – got	do – did	take – took
leave – left	meet – met	swim – swam
make – made	give – gave	eat – ate
see – saw	say – said	tell – told
drink – drank	lose – lost	find – found
write – wrote	buy – bought	forget – forgot
read – read	bring – brought	ride – rode

불규칙 동사의 경우, 과거형이 '–ed'로 끝나지 않고, 각 동사마다 불규칙하게 변한단다. 불규칙 동사의 과거형은 반드시 외워두자.

GRAM CHECK UP

Complete the sentences to make the past tense.

1 We _____ a big bag last week. | buy |

2 I _____ many pictures yesterday. | take |

3 Sandy _____ seafood last night. | eat / not |

4 I _____ at the beach yesterday. | swim / not |

RAM PRACTICE

A. Match and make the correct expressions.

1
go

2
write

3
buy

4
swim

5
take

6
eat

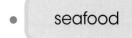 • seafood

• a gift

• a picture

• shopping

• a postcard

• at the beach

B. Correct the mistakes in red and rewrite the sentences.

1 I write a postcard to Jason yesterday.

→ _____.

2 My sister swims at the beach last weekend.

→ _____.

3 We didn't went to the airport by bus.

→ _____.

4 Last winter we taked many pictures in Guam.

→ _____.

5 I didn't bought gifts at the market.

→ _____.

My Fantastic Trip To San Diego!

My name is Ray.
Last summer I went to San Diego with my uncle.
It was a nice city.
My uncle and I swam at the beach every day.
We took a boat and saw whales in the sea.
Sometimes we ate seafood.
We went shopping and bought some gifts.
I had a really good time there.

uncle 삼촌   city 도시   take a boat 배를 타다   whale 고래   sometimes 가끔

1 Did Ray go to San Diego last summer?

_____

2 What did Ray see in the sea?

_____

3 Did he buy books?

_____

 **Read and complete the answers using the given hints.**

You are at the train station. You didn't bring your train ticket. You need the seat number. You left it on your desk. If you call your mom now, what would you say to your mom?

 What would you say to your mom?

Word Box

bring

leave

the seat number

A: Mom, I need your help. I _____ my train ticket.
I _____ it on my desk. Please tell me _____.

 **Look and complete the sentences using the correct forms of the given verbs.**

1

The boy _____ go to Gyeongju last week.

He _____ take pictures with his friends.

2

Later, he _____ go back to the bus.

However, he _____ not, bring his camera.

3

His teacher _____ bring his camera.

He _____ say to her, "Thank you."

Memory Game

Cut out the cards and put them face down.

During your turn, turn over 2 cards. If you turn over a pair, make a sentence using the past tense verbs.

The player with the most cards at the end of the game is the winner.

take a picture

swim at the beach

write a postcard

buy a gift

leave home

go to the airport

eat seafood

see whales

drink orange juice

have a good time

Did You Have A Good Time?

  ☐ **Listen**   ☐ **Repeat**   ☐ **Role play**   ☐ **Chant**

Did you take a field trip today?

Yes, I did.

Where did you go?

I went to the aquarium.

What did you see?

I saw fish, turtles, and dolphins.

Did you have a good time?

Yes, I did.

 **Listen and number the pictures in order.**

zoo

fire station

museum

TV station

aquarium

amusement park

G RAM POINT Did ~? / What Did ~?

- We put **did** before the subject to make a question in the simple past.
  We should put the **verb** after the subject.

Did	I / he / she / it / we / you / they	go	to the zoo?

- We answer with [Yes, (- did).] or [No, (- didn't).]

  Ex Q: Did you go to the zoo?   A: Yes, I did. / No, I didn't.

- We put **what** before [did + the subject].

What did	I / he / she / it / we / you / they	see	at the zoo?

- We answer with [Yes, (- did).] or [No, (- didn't).]

  Ex A: What did you see at the zoo? B: I saw many animals.

> 질문의 형태에 따라 대답의 형태도 달라져! 'what'같은 의문사가 없는 경우에는 'Yes/No'를 사용하여 대답하지만, 의문사가 있는 경우에는 'Yes/No'로 대답해서는 안 된다는 점을 알아두자!

08

G RAM CHECK UP   Look and write *did* or *didn't*.

1

Q: Did you go on the rides?

A: Yes, I _____.

2

Q: Did Nick feed a horse?

A: No, he _____.

3

Q: Did you see the paintings?

A: No, we _____.

4

Q: Did they have a good time?

A: Yes, they _____.

 **A. Match the pictures with the correct words.**

1

2

3

4

5

TV station

amusement park

museum

fire station

aquarium

B. Unscramble the given words.

1 _____ many animals in the zoo?

   you / see / Did

2 _____ to the science museum.

   go / My class / didn't

3 _____ do at the museum?

   did / you / What

4 _____ your friends?

   When / you / meet / did

5 _____ for your field trip?

   Where / go / you / did

 **Read and answer the questions.**

Fun! Fun! Field Trip

Yesterday I took a field trip.
I went to the zoo. It's my favorite place!
What did I see? I saw many
interesting animals.
I especially liked the parrots.
One parrot was good at singing.
It was so cute.
What did I do after lunch?
I had a chance to feed a horse.
Did I have a good time?
Yes, I did. It was so exciting.

favorite 가장 좋아하는   especially 특히   parrot 앵무새   be good at ~을 잘하다   feed 먹이를 주다

1 Did the girl go to the zoo?

_____

2 What did the girl like especially?

_____

3 Did the girl feed an elephant?

_____

GRAM **SPEAKING**   **Look and make a story with the correct forms for each verb.**

A   B

C   D

E   F

A: The boy _____ (meet) his friends for the field trip yesterday.

B: They _____ (take) the bus and _____ (go) to the amusement park.

C: They _____ (go) on many rides and _____ (enjoy) themselves.

D: They _____ (eat) sandwiches for lunch.

E: They _____ (watch) a parade and _____ (take) pictures.

F: They _____ (have) a really good time.

GRAM **WRITING**   **Write an email asking your friend about his/her field trip to the museum using the given expressions.**

Hi Mason,

Did you take a field trip to the museum?

_____ to the museum? Last week?

_____ a good time?

_____ at the museum?

_____ many paintings?

Tell me about your field trip.

| Did you see | Did you have | What did you do | When did you go |

Finding Willy

Find and circle Willy in the picture.

Then, ask and answer the questions based on the picture.

Did Willy go to the zoo?

Yes, he did. / No, he didn't.

zoo
museum
TV station
aquarium
amusement park

I Am Making Cookies

 GRAM TALK Track 33 ☐ Listen ☐ Repeat ☐ Role play

Are you eating lunch?

No. I am cooking.

I am making cookies.

Can you cook well?

Yes! Of course!

But the problem is…

It is not tasty.

 **GRAM Expressions** Track 34 Listen and number the pictures in order. Track 35

swim

cook

draw a picture

collect shells

take a photo

play the piano

• We use am/are/is + (verb) –ing to express that an activity is happening right now.

We should use am/are/is not + (verb) –ing for the negative form.

	Positive	Negative	(Verb) – ing
I	am	am not	watching a movie **now**.
We / You / They	are	are not (aren't)	
He / She / It	is	is not (isn't)	

현재진행형이란 '지금 ~하고 있는 중이다'라는 뜻인데, 현재 진행 중인 동작이나 상태를 나타내지. 기본 문장은 '주어+ am/are/is + 동사 + – ing' 이고, 부정표현은 be동사인 'am/are/is' 뒤에 'not'을 붙이면 돼.

• We add –ing to a verb to form the present continuous.

–ing	watch – watch**ing** play – play**ing** run – run**n**ing draw – draw**ing** collect – collect**ing** swim – swim**m**ing cook – cook**ing** read – read**ing** cut – cut**t**ing
(–e) → (–e̶) –ing	come – com**ing** make – mak**ing** take – tak**ing** write – writ**ing** ride – rid**ing** shine – shin**ing**
(–ie) → y + –ing	lie – l**ying** die – d**ying**

동사를 진행형으로 만들 때는 동사원형에 '~ing'를 붙여주면 돼. 그런데 어떤 동사들은 약간의 변화를 주고 '~ing'를 붙이기도 한단다. 위의 표를 보고 잘 기억해야 해!

 **A. Match the pictures with the words. Then write the correct forms of –ing.**

1 •   • take a photo → _____

2 •   • swim → _____

3 •   • cook → _____

4 •   • play the piano → _____

5 •   • draw a picture → _____

B. Change the sentences as shown in the example.

> Pat plays the violin.   →   Pat is playing the violin.
> →   Pat is not playing the violin.

1   I take photos at the zoo. → _____

→ _____

2   Nick swims in the river. → _____

→ _____

3   We draw pictures. → _____

→ _____

Who Am I?

My name is Ted.
Now I am in the park.
I am wearing a baseball cap.
I am not singing.
I am not eating a hamburger.
I am not listening to music.
I am not reading a book
on the bench.
I am not playing basketball
with my friends.
I am taking a photo using
a cell phone.
Yes! It's me.

baseball cap 야구모자   hamburger 햄버거   bench 벤치   basketball 농구   cell phone 휴대전화

GRAM COMPREHENSION

1 Is Ted wearing a baseball cap?

_____

2 Is Ted listening to music?

_____

3 Is Ted taking a photo with a cellphone?

_____

GRAM SPEAKING

Read and complete the answers using the given hints.

1 Q: What are you doing?   am / read books

A: _____

2 Q: What book are you reading now?   The Ugly Duckling / now

A: _____

3 Q: Where are you going?   am / go to the bookstore

A: _____

4 Q: Who are you going with?   am / go with Sam

A: _____

GRAM WRITING

Write a descriptive sentence using the given hints.

1    collect shells / at the beach

_____

2    make a robot / at home

_____

3    listen to music / in her room

_____

Hobby Board Game

Cut out the cards. Shuffle and put the cards in a pile face down. During your turn, flip a coin.

Heads = move one space / Tails = two spaces

When you land on " 🌼 " you take a card from the top of the pile, then make the sentence. (For example, *He is riding a bike.* / *He is not riding a bike*.)

If your sentence is right, don't move. If your sentence is wrong, move back one space.

Unit 10

I Was Doing My Homework

 GRAM Expressions Track 38 ABC Listen and number the pictures in order. Track 39

do homework

learn Taekwondo

take a walk

read a book

ride a bike

take a piano lesson

GRAM POINT: Was/Were (Not) + (Verb)-ing

- We use **was/were** + (verb) **–ing** to express that an activity was happening at a point of time in the past.

  We should use **was/were not** + (verb) **–ing** for the negative form.

	Positive	Negative	(Verb) – ing
I / He / She / It	was	was not (wasn't)	watching a movie **at 4:00**.
We / You / They	were	were not (weren't)	

- We use the past continuous with phrases like 'at 4:00', 'then', or 'at that time'.

Ex I was watching TV then.

 We weren't playing soccer at that time.

과거진행형은 '~하고 있었다'의 뜻으로, 과거 어느 시점에 진행 중이었던 동작이나 상태를 나타낼 때 사용해!

GRAM CHECK UP

Look and choose the correct words.

1

I was / wasn't riding a bike.

2

They were / weren't playing baseball.

3

Nancy was / wasn't doing homework

4

We were / weren't reading books at home.

A. Write the correct phrases starting with the given letters.

1 do h_____

2 I_____ Taekwondo

3 take a w_____

4 r_____ a book

5 take a piano l_____

6 r_____ a bike

B. Choose the correct words.

1 I [am] [was] watching TV at home then.

2 They [are] [were] watching a movie at 4:00 yesterday.

3 Nick and I [wasn't] [weren't] studying for the test.

4 Angela [was] [were] buying a book there.

5 Kevin and Alex [was] [were] playing badminton.

6 We [wasn't] [weren't] taking an English lesson at that moment.

7 My brother [was] [wasn't] eating dinner. He was sleeping.

8 You [were] [weren't] playing games. You weren't studying.

A New Friend, Alex

Dear Diary,

I made a new friend today.

I was going to the library at 3:20.

It started to rain.

I ran into a store.

I was standing in front of the store at 3:30.

My classmate Alex saw me.

He was going home then.

He was holding an umbrella.

He shared his umbrella with me.

"Thank you, Alex."

make a new friend 새로운 친구를 사귀다 rain 비가 내리다 in front of ~앞에	
classmate 반 친구 hold 들다 share 함께 쓰다	

GRAM COMPREHENSION

1 Was the girl going home at 3:20?

_____

2 Was Alex going to the library at 3:30?

_____

3 Was Alex holding an umbrella?

_____

RAM SPEAKING Look and make a story with the correct words in the sentences.

A  **B**  **C**  **D**  **E**

A Mark was [played] [playing] basketball in the park.

B He [threw] [throwing] the basketball to his friend.

C A girl was [walked] [walking] near them.

D Mark [shouted] [shouting] to her, but she couldn't hear it.

E She was [listened] [listening] to music.

 **RAM WRITING** Write an email giving an apology to your friend using the given expressions.

Hi Erika,

I'm sorry. I _____ a movie with you this afternoon.

I _____ Taekwondo at four o'clock.

You _____ me at 9 o'clock, but I couldn't talk to you.

I _____ a shower then.

Can we meet on Saturday?

Amy

called   didn't watch   was taking   was learning

Tic Tac Toe

Make the sentences using the pictures and phrases.

For example, *I was watching TV. / I was not watching TV.*

If you make a sentence, draw an X or O over the picture.

When you get 4 pictures in a row in any direction, you will get one point.

watch TV

play soccer

play baseball

ride a bike

do homework

learn Taekwondo

watch a movie

take a walk

take a piano lesson

brush one's teeth

buy a book

play badminton

eat dinner

wash one's face

read a book

take a shower

10

Are You Cleaning Your Room?

Greta, where are you?

I am in my room.

Are you cleaning your room?

Yes, I am.

Gram, where are you?

I am in the yard.

Are you watering the plants?

Of course, I am.

 Track 42   Listen and number the pictures in order. Track 43

set the table

clean the room

water the plants

do the dishes

vacuum the floor

take out the trash

• We should put Am/Are/Is before the subject to make a question.

Present	Past	(Subject)	(Verb – ing)
Am	Was	I	
Is		he / she / it	watching a movie?
Are	Were	we / you / they	

• We should answer with "Yes" or "No".

Ex Q1: Are you washing the dishes?

A1: Yes, I am. / No, I am not.

Q2: Were you washing the dishes?

A2: Yes, I was. / No, I wasn't.

'지금 ~하고 있는 중이니?' 또는 '~하고 있는 중이었니?' 하고 의문문을 만들 때는 be 동사와 주어의 위치만 바꿔주면 돼. 대답할 때는 질문의 시제와 같이 'Yes, 주어+be 동사' 또는 'No, 주어+be동사+not'으로 대답한다는 것도 기억하자!

11

GRAM CHECK UP   Unscramble the words to complete the sentences.

1 A: _____ setting / Is / Jack   the table?

B: Yes, he is.

2 A: _____ you / Were / taking   out the trash?

B: No, I wasn't.

3 A: _____ Was / watering / Jean   the plants?

B: No, she wasn't.

4 A: _____ Are / washing / they   the dishes?

B: Yes, they are.

 **A. Match and make the correct expressions.**

1  vacuum

2  water

3  do

4  clean

5  set

6  take out

• the table

• the room

• the trash

• the plants

• the floor

• the dishes

B. Correct the mistakes in red and rewrite the sentences.

1 Are Jason taking out the trash?

➡ _____.

2 Were you water the plants then?

➡ _____.

3 Do you setting the table?

➡ _____.

4 Q: Was your brother washing the window? A: No, he is.

➡ _____.

5 Was you vacuuming the floor?

➡ _____.

Please Help Your Mom!

Last Saturday was Mom's birthday.
So, we wanted to help her all day.
Was Dad vacuuming the floor? Yes, he was.
Was my sister washing the dishes? Yes, she was.
Was my brother cleaning his room? Yes, he was.
Was my pet taking out the trash? Yes, he was.
Then, was I cleaning too? No, I wasn't.
But, I was cooking dinner for my family.
We had a birthday party!
"Happy birthday, Mom!"

all day 하루 종일   pet 애완 동물

1 Was his sister cleaning her room?

_____

2 Was his dad vacuuming the floor?

_____

3 Was he taking out the trash?

_____

GRAM SPEAKING   Look and answer the questions using the given hints.

1

Is the girl setting the table?

_____

water the plants

2

Was the boy taking out the trash?

_____

clean his room

3

What is the girl doing now?

_____

do the dishes

GRAM WRITING   Look and complete the sentences using the given hints.

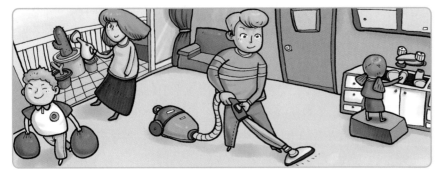

Word Box

washing the dishes
vacuuming the floor
watering the plants
taking out the trash

There are some people in the house.

1 The man is _____.

2 The woman is _____.

3 The boy is _____.

4 The girl is _____.

Coin Flick Game

Flick a coin onto the pictures. Then, ask and answer using the given phrases.

Ex [present / O / clean the room]
Q: Are you cleaning the room?
A: Yes, I am.

set the table

clean the room

vacuum the floor

watch a movie

water the plants

do the dishes

take out the trash

cook dinner

watch TV

Unit 12 — What Was He Doing?

 **G**RAM **Expressions** Track 46 **A**B**C** Listen and number the pictures in order. Track 47

sing
in the chorus

interview

play music

see the stars

exercise

watch a
movie

• We put what, where, etc. before be verb(am/are/is or was/were) in present continuous or past continuous questions.

	Present	Past		watching?
What Where	am	was	I	
	is		he / she / it	
	are	were	we / you / they	

• We should answer without "Yes" or "No".

Ex Q1: What were you doing?

A1: I was watching an action movie.

Q2: Where were you watching a movie?

A2: I was watching a movie at home.

'Who'나 'what'같은 의문사가 있는 현재 또는 과거진행형의 의문문에서는 의문사를 문장 맨 앞에 놓고, 그 뒤에 순서대로 'be동사+주어+동사 −ing'가 나오게 되지. 의문사가 있는 의문문에서는 'Yes/No'로 대답하지 않는다는 점 꼭 기억하자!

G RAM CHECK UP — Look and write the correct word.

Word Box	practicing	singing
	playing	writing

1

A: What is Ray doing?

B: He is _____ in the band.

2

A: What was Susie doing?

B: She was _____ in the choir.

3

A: What are you doing?

B: I am _____ for the school newspaper.

4

A: What are they doing?

B: They are _____ English.

A. Write the correct phrases starting with the given letters.

1

i_____

2

sing in the c_____

3

see the s_____

4

play m_____

5

e_____

6

w_____ a m_____

B. Read and complete the sentences using *What* or *Where*.

1 A: _____ are you making?

B: I am making a new robot.

2 A: _____ are you going?

B: We are going to the science room.

3 A: _____ were they singing?

B: They were singing Arirang.

4 A: _____ was Cindy doing in the play?

B: She was acting the princess.

5 A: _____ is Maggie reading a book?

B: She is reading a book in the library.

Read and answer the questions. Track 48

What Was I Doing?

I met Nina after class.
She was holding a large box.
I asked her, "Where are you going?"
She was going to her magic club.
I helped her and we went to her club.
Some students were learning magic from
a teacher.
Nina told me, "Join my magic club,"
and I did.
What was I doing?
I was learning MAGIC!

| magic 마술   hold 들다   join 가입하다 |

G RAM
COMPREHENSION

1 What was Nina holding?

_____

2 Where was Nina going?

_____

3 Was the boy learning magic?

_____

GRAM **SPEAKING** Unscramble the questions.

1 Q: _____   you / going / were / Where / ?

A: I was going to the library.

2 Q: _____   there / ? / doing / What / were / you

A: I was reading a book.

3 Q: _____   library / Who / in / the / were / ?

A: There were many students in the library.

4 Q: _____   they / ? / doing / were / What

A: They were studying for the test .

GRAM **WRITING** Look and make questions using the given hints.

1    **2**    **3**

1 Q: _____   where / go

A: She was going to the music room.

2 Q: _____   who / talk with

A: She was talking with her music teacher.

3 Q: _____   what / do

A: The students were waiting for their teacher.

FUNNY GRAM

Matching Game

Cut out the cards and put them face down.

Turn over 2 cards. If you turn over a pair, you can put them on the board. Then ask and answer the questions using the given pronouns and phrases.

What was she doing?

She was playing music.

Put the picture card here.

Put the picture card here.

12

It Is Under The Desk

GRAM Expressions Track 50 ABC Listen and number the pictures in order. Track 51

on the wall   behind the desk   under the chair   in the closet   in front of the computer

G RAM POINT It / On / Under / In front of / Behind

- We use in, on, under, in front of, or behind before a noun to show places.

 in the box

 on the box

 under the box

 in front of the box

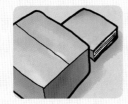 behind the box

장소를 나타내는 전치사에는 'in (~안에)', 'on (~위에)', 'under (~아래에)', 'in front of (~앞에)', 'behind (~뒤에)' 등이 있어. 각 전치사의 뜻을 잘 구별하여 알아두자.

G RAM CHECK UP

Look and write *in, on, under, in front of* – or *behind*.

1

The doll is _____ the desk.

2

The cat is _____ the piano.

3

The chairs are _____ the bed.

4

The hats are _____ the box.

5

The bookshelf is _____ the desk.

6

The English book is _____ the chair.

 **A. Look and write the words you can see in the pictures.**

bed	doll	floor	~~map~~	TV	bookshelf
closet	~~wall~~	box	hat	window	backpack

1

map

wall

2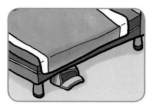

3

4

5

6

B. Look at the pictures and correct the mistakes.

1

The shirt is under the closet.

_____.

2

The TV is behind the window.

_____.

3

The cups are in the bookshelf.

_____.

4

The backpack is on the chair.

_____.

5

The desks are on the window.

_____.

Welcome To My Room!

My name is Rick.
I have a big desk and a chair in my room.
The computer is on the desk.
The small printer is behind the computer.
The two bookshelves are next to the desk.
I have many books.
My bed is in front of the window.
Many toy boxes are under the bed.
My room is not big, but I really like it.

welcome 환영하다   printer 프린터   bookshelves 책장(bookshelf)의 복수형   next to ~옆에   many 많은

GRAM **COMPREHENSION**

1 Where is Rick's computer?

_____

2 Are Rick's toy boxes next to the bookshelves?

_____

3 Where are Rick's toy boxes?

_____

Read and complete the answers using the given hints.

1 Q: Do you have a window in your room?

A: _____
[have / a big window]

2 Q: Where is your desk?

A: _____
[in front of / the window]

3 Q: Where is your bed?

A: _____
[next to / the desk]

4 Q: Where is your computer?

A: _____
[on / the desk]

Write an email telling your friend about your room using the given picture and expressions.

Hi Sarah,

Today I will tell you about my room.

I have a big window.

I have a desk and a chair (1) _____.

My small bookshelf is (2) _____.

I have many dolls (3) _____.

I have a big world map (4) _____, too.

on the wall   on the desk   under the bed   in front of the window

In My Room

Put the stickers in the right place.

▶ hat in the closet

▶ map on the wall

▶ doll under the bed

▶ chair in front of the piano

▶ window behind the desk

▶ box under the chair

▶ computer on the desk

▶ printer behind the computer

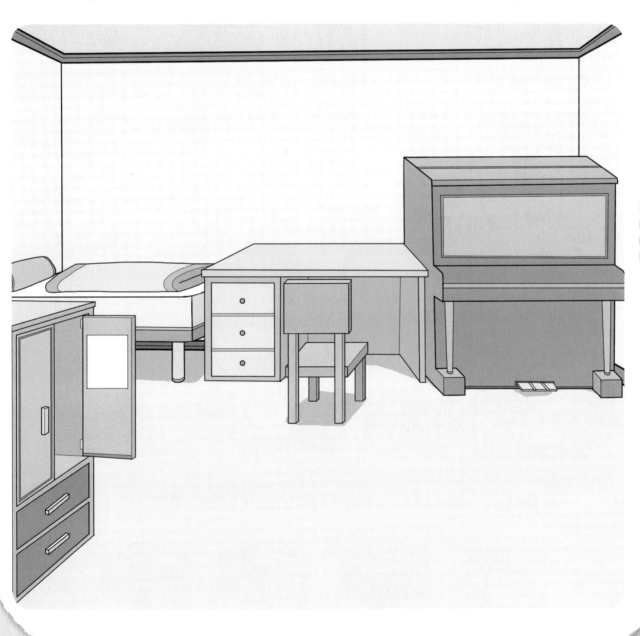

13

It Is Next To The Hospital

GRAM TALK (Track 53) □ Listen □ Repeat □ Role play

GRAM Expressions (Track 54) ABC Listen and number the pictures in order. (Track 55)

post office

hospital

movie theater

police station

bank

fire station

Next To / Between / Across From

• We use next to, between, or across from before a noun to show places or positions.

1   2   3

장소를 나타낼 때 사용되는 전치사에는 'next to (~옆에)', 'between ~ and ~ (~사이에)', 그리고 'across from (~건너편에)' 등이 있어. 각 전치사들의 뜻을 잘 구별하여 알아두자.

Where is the post office?

(1) The post office is next to the bank.

(2) The post office is between the bank and the police station.

(3) The post office is across from the hospital.

GRAM
CHECK UP

Look and write *next to, between,* or *across from.*

1

The bank is _____ the hospital.

2

The police station is _____ the park.

3

The hospital is _____ the park and the bank.

4

The fire station is _____ the police station.

14

RAM PRACTICE A. Write the correct words starting with the given letters.

1

p_____

2

b_____

3

h_____

4

p_____ s_____

5

f_____ s_____

6

movie t_____

B. Read the sentences and write the correct names in the map.

- The bank is between the hotel and the restaurant.
- The post office is across from the bank.
- The police station is across from the restaurant.
- The movie theater is next to the post office.

1 [_____]

2 [_____]

3 [_____]

4 [_____]

Around My School

The library is next to my school.
I go to the library after school.
The Grace Park is across from
my school.
I ride a bike with my friends
in the park.
I love to go to Anne's Pizza.
It is between the Grace Park and
the post office.
We enjoy the delicious pizza there.

around ~주변에   ride 타다   bike 자전거   enjoy 즐기다   delicious 맛있는

GRAM COMPREHENSION

1 Where is the library?

_____

2 Where is the Grace Park?

_____

3 Where is Anne's Pizza?

_____

 **Look and answer the questions using the given hints.**

 **1** Is the bank next to the library?

_____

across from

 **2** Where is the post office?

_____

the bank / between / the restaurant

 **3** Is the hospital across from the police station?

_____

next to

  **Look and complete the sentences using the given hints.**

 **1** The library is _____.

next to

 **2** The restaurant is _____.

between

 **3** The park is _____.

across from

Place the buildings anywhere you want.
Then, say the sentences using "next to, between, across from."
(For example, "The bank is *next to* the market.")

Unit 15 There Is A Zoo In My Town

  RAM TALK (Track 57) ☐ Listen ☐ Repeat ☐ Role play

Let me introduce my town to you.

Is there a zoo in your town?

Yes, there is a large zoo in my town.

There is a beautiful park next to the zoo.

Are there many trees in the park?

Yes, there are.

Also, there are many supermarkets in my town.

I never want to move!

RAM Expressions (Track 58) **ABC** Listen and number the pictures in order. (Track 59)

museum

concert hall

fish market

train station

old palace

library

There + Be Verbs

- We use there + is (are) to express that something is in a particular place.
  We should use is before the singular subject and are before the plural subject.

	Positive	Negative	(Subject)	
There	is	is not (isn't)	a park	in my town.
	are	are not (aren't)	two parks	

- We put is (are) before there to make a question.

Ex Q: Is there a concert hall in your town?

A: Yes, there is. / No, there isn't.

'There is(are)~'는 '~이 있다'라는 뜻이야. 문장의 주어는 맨 앞에 나오는 'there'가 아니라 be동사 뒤에 나오는 명사라는 것이 특징이지. 주어가 단수일 때는 'is'를, 주어가 복수일 때는 'are'를 쓴다는 점도 잊지 말자!

GRAM **CHECK UP** Look and write *is* or *are*.

1

There _____ a fish market in my town.

2

There _____ many people in the library.

3

There _____ many banks in my town.

4

There _____ a concert hall next to the park.

 **A. Match the pictures with the correct words.**

1  **2** **3**  **4**  **5**

• • • • •

• • • • •

| library | old palace | concert hall | train station | fish market |

B. Complete the sentences with the given words.

1 _____ in my town.

a concert hall / isn't / there

2 _____ in the town.

old palaces / there / aren't

3 _____ next to the park?

there / a library / is

4 _____ across from City Hall.

there / a museum / is

5 _____ in the concert hall?

are / many people / there

 **Read and answer the questions.**

My Favorite Place In My Town

My favorite place in my town is the
children's library.
There are a lot of interesting
books in the library.
There are special reading
programs for children.
There is a small movie theater
for children, too.
I love to see movies with my
friends there.
There is a beautiful garden
in front of the library.
Is there a children's library in your town?

| favorite 가장 좋아하는 a lot of 많은 special 특별한 reading program 독서프로그램 |

1 Are there reading programs in the library?

_____

2 Is there a movie theater in the library?

_____

3 Is there a park in front of the library?

_____

GRAM SPEAKING

Complete the sentences with *is* or *are*. Then look and number the sentences in order.

A  B  C  D  E

A There _____ two interesting places in my town.

☐ There _____ a famous fish market in my town.

☐ There _____ many big trees in the palace.

☐ There _____ an old palace in my town, too.

☐ There _____ many people in the market every day.

GRAM WRITING

 Look and complete the sentences using the given words and phrases.

There are some people in the museum.

1 There _____ _____ on the wall.

2 There _____ _____ in front of the painting.

3 There _____ _____ on the bench.

4 There _____ _____ next to the door.

Word Box   is   are   a woman   a large painting   a man and a girl   two boys

My Town

Flip a coin.

Heads = move one space / Tails = two spaces

Then, say the sentences like "*There is a big museum in my town*." If you are right, don't move. If not, move back one space.

Where Is The Bakery?

 Track 62 Listen and number the pictures in order. Track 63

| bakery | clothing store | ice cream shop | bookstore | supermarket | stationery store |

GRAM POINT Where

- We use where to ask a question about a place.

  Ex Q: Where is the bookstore?   A: It is across from the bank.

- We use where to ask directions. The following expressions are used when we give directions.

go straight   turn left   turn right

의문사 'where'는 '어디'라는 뜻으로 장소를 물을 때 사용해. 어떤 장소가 어디에 있는지 묻고 답할 때 자주 사용되는 표현을 알아두자!

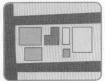   

block   at the corner   on your left   on your right

GRAM CHECK UP

Look and write the correct words.

1

The supermarket is on your _____.

2

Go _____ and turn _____.

3

Go _____ and turn _____.

4

The bookstore is at the _____.

16

A. Match the pictures with the correct words.

1  •   • supermarket •   •

2  •   • bakery •   •

3  •   • bookstore •   •

4  •   • stationery store •   •

5  •   • ice cream shop •   •

B. Look and answer the questions with the given phrases.

1 Q: Where is the bank?

A: It is _____ the bakery.

2 Q: Where is the ice cream shop?

A: It is _____.

3 Q: Where is the bookstore?

A: It is _____ the supermarket.

4 Q: Where is the supermarket?

A: Go straight one block and _____. It is on your left.

5 Q: Where is the stationery store?

A: Go straight one block and _____. It is on your left.

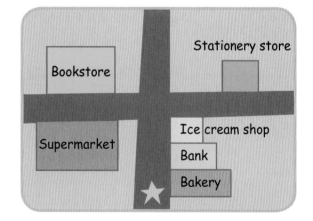

Word Box

next to
across from
at the corner
turn right
turn left

GRAM READING **Read and answer the questions.** Track 64

Come To My House!

This Saturday is my birthday.
Come to my house.
It is next to the stationery store.
I will tell you how you get to my house.
Look at the map on this invitation card.
Start at the school.

Go straight one block.
There is a bank at the corner.
Turn left at the corner. Go straight.
My house is on your left.
See you this Saturday.

stationery store 문방구	get to ~에 도착하다	start 시작하다	map 지도	invitation card 초대장

GRAM COMPREHENSION

1 Where is the girl's house?

_____

2 Where is the bank?

_____

3 How to get to the girl's house?

_____

 **Read and complete the answers using the given phrases.**

A girl asks you, "Where is an ice cream shop?" Look at the map and give directions. What would you say to her?

Where is an ice cream shop?

An ice cream shop is _____ the bookstore. _____ and turn right _____.

[go straight / next to / at the corner]

 **Look and complete the sentences using the given phrases.**

1

2

3

| Word Box | turn left | stationery store | next to | notebook |

1 On the way to the library, Jay needed a _____ and a pencil.

2 He asked a girl, "Where is the _____?"

3 She told him, "It is _____ the bakery.

Go straight and _____."

FUNNY GRAM

Giving Directions

Prepare the markers for the players. Then at his or her turn, move the marker and say where the marker is landed. You can use the expressions below.

▶ Go straight _____ block.

▶ Turn _____.

▶ There is _____ at the corner.

▶ Turn _____ at the corner.

▶ It is on your _____.

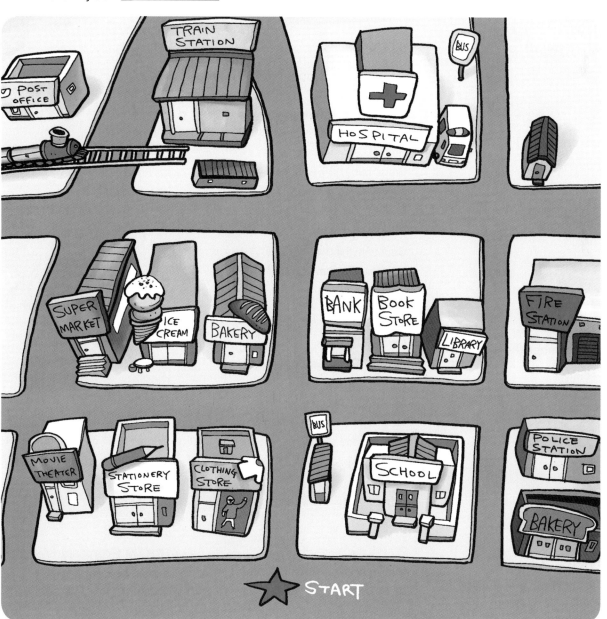

Audio Script

GRAM GRAM PLUS Book3

[Track 1] p.8

Unit 01. Can You Play Soccer?

Listen to the dialogue.

Boy: Can you play soccer?
Gram: Yes, I can.
Gram: I can kick the ball.
Gram: I can pass the ball, too.
Boy: Can you score a goal, too?
Gram: No, I can't.
Boy: Oh, my!

[Track 2]

[GRAM Expressions]

Listen and repeat.
play soccer
play tennis
play basketball
play volleyball
play baseball
play badminton

[Track 03]

Listen and number the pictures in order.
1. play basketball
2. play soccer
3. play baseball
4. play tennis
5. play badminton
6. play volleyball

[Track 04] p.11

[GRAM READING]

Listen to the story and answer the questions.
-I Like Sports!-
My name is Jason.

I really like sports.
I can play basketball.
I play basketball three times a week.
I can play basketball at the gym.

When I play basketball, I can pass the ball.
I can bounce the ball, too.
But, I can't shoot the ball well.
So, I can't score points.
I'm going to practice every day.

[Track 05] p.14

Unit 02. You Should Wear A Helmet

Listen to the dialogue.
Boy: Let's in-line skate tomorrow.
Gram: Good idea!
Gram: Should I wear a helmet?
Boy: Yes, you should.
Gram: Should I wear knee pads, too?
Boy: Yes, you should.
Gram: Anything else?
Boy: You shouldn't be late.
Gram: OK.

[Track 06]

[GRAM Expressions]

Listen and repeat.
wear a helmet
be late
take off shoes
wear knee pads
be quiet
play computer games

[Track 07]

Listen and number the pictures in order.
1. be quiet
2. take off shoes
3. be late
4. play computer games
5. wear a helmet
6. wear knee pads

[Track 08] p.17

[GRAM READING]

Listen to the story and answer the questions.
-Let's Go Camping-
Dear Alice,
My family will go hiking up the mountain.
Let's go together.
You should bring your hiking boots. You should bring a hat and warm clothes, too.
My mother will cook, so you shouldn't bring a lunch.
You should come to my house by nine o'clock on Saturday.
You shouldn't be late.
See you on Saturday.
Cindy

[Track 09] p.20

Unit 03. You Must Speak In English

Listen to the dialogue.
Gram: Are you new here?
Girl: Yes.
Girl: Please tell me the class rules.
Gram: OK.
Gram: First, you must not be late.
Gram: You must speak in English.
Gram: You must not be noisy in class.

[Track 10]

[GRAM Expressions]

Listen and repeat.
be late
litter
run

be noisy

fight

cheat

[Track 11]

Listen and number the pictures in order.

1. run
2. fight
3. cheat
4. be late
5. litter
6. be noisy

[Track 12] p.23

[GRAM READING]

Listen to the story and answer the questions.

-Please Follow The School Rules-

Good morning, students.

I'm Mr. Henson. I will tell you three school rules. You must follow them.

First, you must not make fun of your classmates.

Second, you must not talk loudly in the library. You must be quiet there.

Third, you must not litter in school.

You must put the trash in the trash can.

Please follow the rules.

[Track 13] p.26

Unit 04. You Have To Be On Time

Listen to the dialogue.

Greta: You have to be on time.

Gram: Sorry.

Greta: You have to eat slowly.

Greta: You have to chew with your mouth closed.

Greta: You have to ask me to pass the salt.

Greta: You have to…

Gram: You have to be quiet.

[Track 14]

[GRAM Expressions]

Listen and repeat.

be on time

wait one's turn

ask to pass the salt

give up one's seat

cover one's mouth

[Track 15]

Listen and number the pictures in order.

1. ask to pass the salt
2. be on time
3. cover one's mouth
4. give up one's seat
5. wait one's turn

[Track 16] p.29

[GRAM READING]

Listen to the story and answer the questions.

-Enjoy The Movie!-

Attention, students.

I have tickets for you, so you don't have to buy tickets.

When you get a ticket, you have to check your seat numbers.

Before the movie starts, you have to turn off your cell phones.

You have to talk quietly during the movie.

Please don't be noisy.

Enjoy the movie.

[Track 17] p.32

Unit 05. The Party Was Great!

Listen to the dialogue

Girl: How was your Christmas?

Gram: It was great!

Girl: Were you at home?

Gram: No, I wasn't.

Gram: I was at Jason's Christmas party.

Gram: The Christmas music was good.

Gram: The food was delicious, too.

[Track 18]

[GRAM Expressions]

Listen and repeat.

Christmas

Thanksgiving

New Year's Day

Halloween

Valentine's Day

Children's Day

[Track 19]

Listen and number the pictures in order.

1. Thanksgiving
2. Children's Day
3. New Year's Day
4. Christmas
5. Valentine's Day
6. Halloween

[Track 20] p.35

[GRAM READING]

Listen to the story and answer the questions.

-How Was Your Halloween?-

Last Thursday was Halloween.

My sister and I were at Ben's Halloween party.

The party was so much fun.

The food was delicious.

We had a Halloween costume contest there.

My rabbit costume was good,

but I wasn't the winner.

The winner was Susie.
Her pumpkin costume was so cute.

[Track 21] p.38

Unit 06. My Family Watched A Movie

Listen to the dialogue.
Girl: How was your weekend?
Gram: Great.
Gram: My family watched a movie.
Gram: Then we visited our grandparents.
Gram: We talked about our trip to Busan.
Gram: We arrived home very late.
Gram: I was so tired

[Track 22]
[GRAM Expressions]
Listen and repeat.
watch
play badminton
invite
climb
enjoy
visit

[Track 23]
Listen and number the pictures in order.
1. invite
2. climb
3. enjoy
4. play badminton
5. visit
6. watch

[Track 24] p.41
[GRAM READING]
Listen to the story and answer the questions.
-Surprise Party For Mom!-
My name is Brian.

Last Saturday was my mom's birthday.
My dad and I planned a surprise party for her.
We prepared many balloons.
We invited my mom's friends to the party.
We cooked her favorite food, too.
We turned off the lights and waited for her.
We shouted, "Happy Birthday!" She really liked the party.

[Track 25] p.44

Unit 07. We Took A Trip

Listen to the dialogue.
Girl: Did you go to Jeju?
Gram: Yes. My family took a trip.
Girl: Did you have a good time?
Gram: Yes, we did.
Gram: We swam at the beach.
Girl: Did you eat seafood?
Gram: Yes, we did.
Gram: It was delicious.

[Track 26]
[GRAM Expressions]
Listen and repeat.
take a picture
eat seafood
go shopping
buy a gift
swim at the beach
write a postcard

[Track 27]
Listen and number the pictures in order.
1. swim at the beach
2. buy a gift
3. take a picture
4. write a postcard
5. go shopping
6. eat seafood

[Track 28] p.47
[GRAM READING]
Listen to the story and answer the questions.
-My Fantastic Trip To San Diego!
My name is Ray.
Last summer I went to San Diego with my uncle.
It was a nice city.
My uncle and I swam at the beach every day.
We took a boat and saw whales in the sea.
Sometimes we ate seafood.
We went shopping and bought some gifts.
I had a really good time there.

[Track 29] p.50

Unit 08. Did You Have A Good Time?

Listen to the dialogue.
Dad: Did you take a field trip today?
Gram: Yes, I did.
Dad: Where did you go?
Gram: I went to the aquarium.
Dad: What did you see?
Gram: I saw fish, turtles, and dolphins.
Dad: Did you have a good time?
Gram: Yes, I did.

[Track 30]
[GRAM Expressions]
Listen and repeat.
zoo
fire station
museum
TV station
aquarium
amusement park

[Track 31]

Listen and number the pictures in order.

1. fire station
2. aquarium
3. museum
4. amusement park
5. zoo
6. TV station

[Track 32] p. 53

[GRAM READING]

Listen to the story and answer the questions.

-Fun! Fun! Field Trip-

Yesterday I took a field trip.

I went to the zoo. It's my favorite place!

What did I see? I saw many interesting animals.

I especially liked the parrots.

One parrot was good at singing.

It was so cute.

What did I do after lunch?

I had a chance to feed a horse.

Did I have a good time?

Yes, I did. It was so exciting.

[Track 33] p. 56

Unit 09. I AM Making Cookies

Listen to the dialogue.

Boy: Are you eating lunch?

Gram: No. I am cooking.

Gram: I am making cookies.

Boy: Can you cook well?

Gram: Yes! Of course!

Gram: But the problem is...

Boy: It is not tasty.

[Track 34]

[GRAM Expressions]

Listen and repeat.

swim

cook

draw a picture

collect shells

take a photo

play the piano

[Track 35]

Listen and number the pictures in order.

1. draw a picture
2. play the piano
3. cook
4. collect shells
5. swim
6. take a photo

[Track 36] p. 59

[GRAM READING]

Listen to the story and answer the questions.

-Who Am I?-

My name is Ted.

Now I am in the park.

I am wearing a baseball cap.

I am not singing.

I am not eating a hamburger.

I am not listening to music.

I am not reading a book on the bench.

I am not playing basketball with my friends.

I am taking a photo using a cell phone.

Yes! It's me.

[Track 37] p.62

Unit 10. I Was Doing My Homework

Listen to the dialogue.

Mom: What were you doing?

Gram: I was doing my homework.

Mom: What were you doing?

Gram: I was reading a book.

Gram: Wow, it's fun!

Mom: What were you doing?

Gram: I was playing computer games.

[Track 38]

[GRAM Expressions]

Listen and repeat.

do homework

learn Taekwondo

take a walk

read a book

ride a bike

take a piano lesson

[Track 39]

Listen and number the pictures in order.

1. learn Taekwondo
2. take a piano lesson
3. ride a bike
4. take a walk
5. do homework
6. read a book

[Track 40] p.65

[GRAM READING]

Listen to the story and answer the questions.

-A New Friend, Alex-

Dear Diary,

I made a new friend today.

I was going to the library at 3:20.

It started to rain.

I ran into a store.

I was standing in front of the store at 3:30.

My classmate Alex saw me.

He was going home then.

He was holding an umbrella.

He shared his umbrella with me.

"Thank you, Alex."

Unit 11. Are You Cleaning Your Room?

Listen to the dialogue.

Mom: Greta, where are you?
Greta: I am in my room.
Mom: Are you cleaning your room?
Greta: Yes, I am.
Mom: Gram, where are you?
Gram: I am in the yard.
Mom: Are you watering the plants?
Gram: Of course, I am.

[Track 42]

[GRAM Expressions]

Listen and repeat.

set the table
clean the room
water the plants
do the dishes
vacuum the floor
take out the trash

[Track 43]

Listen and number the pictures in order.

1. water the plants
2. vacuum the floor
3. clean the room
4. take out the trash
5. set the table
6. do the dishes

[Track 44] p.71

[GRAM READING]

Listen to the story and answer the questions.

-Please Help Your Mom!-
Last Saturday was Mom's birthday.
So, we wanted to help her all day.
Was Dad vacuuming the floor?
Yes, he was.

Was my sister washing the dishes?
Yes, she was.
Was my brother cleaning his room?
Yes, he was.
Was my pet taking out the trash?
Yes, he was.
Then, was I cleaning too? No, I wasn't.
But, I was cooking dinner for my family.
We had a birthday party!
"Happy birthday, Mom!"

[Track 45] p.74

Unit 12. What Was He Doing?

Listen to the dialogue.

Girl: Where were you?
Gram: I was in the classroom.
Girl: What were you doing?
Gram: I was reading a book.
Girl: What book were you reading?
Gram: Romeo And Juliet. I have a club meeting today.
Girl: Really?

[Track 46]

[GRAM Expressions]

Listen and repeat.

sing in the chorus
interview
play music
see the stars
exercise
watch a movie

[Track 47]

Listen and number the pictures in order.

1. watch a movie
2. interview
3. see the stars
4. exercise
5. play music
6. sing in the chorus (pause)

[Track 48] p.77

Listen to the story and answer the questions.

-What Was I Doing?-
I met Nina after class.
She was holding a large box.
I asked her, "Where are you going?"
She was going to her magic club.
I helped her and we went to her club.
Some students were learning magic from a teacher.
Nina told me, "Join my magic club," and I did.
What was I doing?
I was learning MAGIC!

[Track 45] p.80

Unit 13. It Is Under The Desk

Listen to the dialogue.

Mom: Are you ready for school?
Gram: No, not yet.
Gram: Where is my backpack?
Mom: It's under the desk.
Gram: Where is my English book?
Mom: It's on the chair.
Gram: Where is my pencil case?
Mom: Isn't it in your backpack?
Gram: Oh, here it is.

[Track 50]

[GRAM Expressions]

Listen and repeat.

on the wall
behind the desk
under the chair
in the closet
in front of the computer

[Track 51]

Listen and number the pictures in order.

1. in the closet
2. in front of the computer

3. under the chair

4. on the wall

5. behind the desk

[Track 52] p.83

[GRAM READING]

Listen to the story and answer the questions.

-Welcome To My Room!-

My name is Rick.

I have a big desk and a chair in my room.

The computer is on the desk.

The small printer is behind the computer.

The two bookshelves are next to the desk.

I have many books.

My bed is in front of the window.

Many toy boxes are under the bed.

My room is not big, but I really like it.

[Track 53] p.86

Unit 14. It Is Next To The Hospital

Listen to the dialogue.

Girl: Excuse me.

Girl: Where is the post office?

Gram: It is next to the hospital.

Girl: Where is the hospital?

Gram: It is across from the bank.

Gram: Follow me. I'll take you to the post office.

Girl: Thank you

[Track 54]

[GRAM Expressions]

Listen and repeat.

post office

hospital

movie theater

police station

bank

fire station

[Track 55]

Listen and number the pictures in order.

1. bank

2. post office

3. fire station

4. movie theater

5. hospital

6. police station

[Track 56] Page 89

[GRAM READING]

Listen to the story and answer the questions.

-Around My School-

The library is next to my school.

I go to the library after school.

The Grace Park is across from my school.

I ride a bike with my friends in the park.

I love to go to Anne's Pizza.

It is between the Grace Park and the post office.

We enjoy the delicious pizza there.

[Track 57] p.92

Unit 15. There Is A Zoo In My Town

Listen to the dialogue.

Gram: Let me introduce my town to you.

Girl: Is there a zoo in your town?

Gram: Yes, there is a large zoo in my town.

Gram: There is a beautiful park next to the zoo.

Girl: Are there many trees in the park?

Gram: Yes, there are.

Gram: Also, there are many supermarkets in my town.

Gram: I never want to move!

[Track 58]

[GRAM Expressions]

Listen and repeat.

museum

concert hall

fish market

train station

old palace

library

[Track 59]

Listen and number the pictures in order.

1. old palace

2. museum

3. fish market

4. concert hall

5. library

6. train station

[Track 60] p.95

[GRAM READING]

Listen to the story and answer the questions.

-My Favorite Place In My Town-

My favorite place in my town is the children's library.

There are a lot of interesting books in the library.

There are special reading programs for children.

There is a small movie theater for children, too.

I love to see movies with my friends there.

There is a beautiful garden in front of the library.

Is there a children's library in your town?

[Track 61] p.98

Unit 16. Where Is The Bakery?

Listen to the dialogue.

Boy: Excuse me. Where is the bakery?

Gram: Bakery?

Gram: Go straight one block.

Gram: Then turn right.

Gram: The bakery is on your left.

Gram: Here we are!

[Track 62]

[GRAM Expressions]

Listen and repeat.

bakery

clothing store

ice cream shop

bookstore

supermarket

stationery store

[Track 63]

Listen and number the pictures in order.

1. bookstore

2. stationery store

3. bakery

4. supermarket

5. ice cream shop

6. clothing store

[Track 64] p.101

[GRAM READING]

Listen to the story and answer the questions.

-Come To My House!-

This Saturday is my birthday.

Come to my house.

It is next to the stationery store.

I will tell you how you get to my house.

Look at the map on this invitation card.

Start at the school.

Go straight one block.

There is a bank at the corner.

Turn left at the corner. Go straight.

My house is on your left.

See you this Saturday.

Answers

Unit 01. Can You Play Soccer?

[GRAM WORDS] p.8

2-4-1-6-3-5

[GRAM CHECK UP] p.9

1. He **can** skate.
2. She **can't** play baseball.
3. He **can't** skate.
4. She **can** play baseball.

[GRAM PRACTICE] p.10

A.

1. play s**occer**
2. play b**asketball**
3. play b**aseball**
4. play b**adminton**
5. play t**ennis**
6. play v**olleyball**

B.

1. Jenny **can't** play soccer.
2. Jason **can** play basketball.
3. April **can** play tennis.
4. Jenny **can't** play basketball.
5. Jason **can't** play tennis.
6. April **can't** play soccer.

[GRAM Comprehension] p.11

1. Yes, he can.
2. Yes, he can.
3. No, he can't.

[GRAM Speaking] p.12

1. I like soccer.
2. Yes, I can play soccer well.
3. I play soccer once a week.
4. I play soccer with my friends.

[GRAM Writing]

1. He can play basketball.

2. She can't ride a bike.
3. He can play volleyball.

Unit 02. You Should Wear A Helmet

[GRAM EXPRESSIONS] p.14

5-3-2-6-1-4

[GRAM CHECK UP] p.15

1. You **shouldn't** be late.
2. You **should** stretch first.
3. You **should** wear knee pads.
4. You **shouldn't** play computer games.

[GRAM PRACTICE] p.16

A.

1. **take off** shoes
2. be **late**
3. **wear** a helmet
4. wear **knee pads**
5. be **quiet**
6. **play** computer games

B.

1. Ryan shouldn't bring knee pads.
2. Angela should bring a helmet.
3. Brian shouldn't bring a swimming hat.

[GRAM Comprehension] p.17

1. Yes, she should.
2. No, she shouldn't.
3. Yes, she should.

[GRAM Speaking] p.18

1. I should go hiking with my father.
2. I should go to the movies with Julie.

[GRAM Writing]

1. You **should wear a helmet and**

knee pads.
2. You **should go to my room and bring them**.
3. You **shouldn't be late**.

Unit 03. You Must Speak In English

[GRAM EXPRESSIONS] p.20

4-5-1-6-2-3

[GRAM CHECK UP] p.21

1. He **mustn't** speak in Korean.
2. She **must** be quiet in class.
3. He **must** speak in English.
4. She **mustn't** be noisy in class.

[GRAM PRACTICE] p.22

A.

1. r**un** in the hallway
2. be n**oisy**
3. be l**ate**
4. c**heat** in the exam
5. l**itter**
6. f**ight** with classmates

B.

1. B / You **must not** run in the hallway.
2. B / You **must not** litter in school.
3. G / You **must** follow the school rules.
4. B / You **must not** fight with classmates.
5. B / You **must not** cheat in the exam.
6. B / You **must not** use a cellphone in class.

[GRAM Comprehension] p.23

1. must → must not / mustn't
2. must not → must
3. must → must not / mustn't

[GRAM Speaking] p.24
(5) She answers, "OK. See you tomorrow."
(1) A new girl comes to class.
(3) In the library, he says to her, "You **must not** be noisy here."
(2) A boy tells her, "You **must not** run in the hallway."
(4) On the way home, he tells her, "You **must not** be late for school."

[GRAM Writing]
1. Susie **must not litter**.
2. Nick **must not use a cellphone at school**.
3. Maggie **must not run in the classroom**.

Unit 04. You Have To Be On Time

[GRAM WORDS] p.26
2-5-1-4-3

[GRAM CHECK UP] p.27
1. I **have to** wear a dress.
2. He **doesn't have to** take off his shoes.
3. I **don't have to** wear a dress.
4. He **has to** take off his shoes.

[GRAM PRACTICE] p.28
A.
1. wait one's t**urn**
2. be on t**ime**
3. ask to p**ass** the salt
4. g**ive** up one's seat
5. c**over** one's mouth

B.
1. He **has** to give up his seat.
2. I have lots of time. I don't **have** to hurry.
3. We **don't** have to wait our turn.
4. I **have** to cover my mouth when coughing.

5. You **have** to chew with your mouth closed.
6. She **doesn't** have to wear a dress to the party.

[GRAM Comprehension] p.29
1. No, they don't have to.
2. Yes, they have to.
3. Yes, they have to.

[GRAM Speaking] p.30
1. Yes. She has to give up her seat.
2. No. They have to be quiet.
3. No. The girl has to turn off her camera.

[GRAM Writing]
1. have to / be on time
2. have to / turn off your cellphone
3. have to / be quiet

Unit 05. The Party Was Great!

[GRAM EXPRESSIONS] p.32
4-1-3-6-5-2

[GRAM CHECK UP] p.33
1. The turkey **was** very delicious.
2. I **was** excited about the sunrise.
3. **Was** the Christmas parade interesting?
4. **Were** your parents happy with the chocolates?

[GRAM PRACTICE] p.34
A.
1. New Year's Day - sunrise
2. Thanksgiving - turkey
3. Christmas - gingerbread
4. Halloween - costume
5. Valentine's Day – chocolate

B.
1. was

2. wasn't
3. were
4. was
5. wasn't
6. was
7. was

[GRAM Comprehension] p.35
1. No, she wasn't. / No, she was at Halloween party.
2. Yes, it was. / Yes, it was so much fun.
3. Yes, it was. / Yes, her pumpkin costume was so cute.

[GRAM Speaking] p.36
1. He was at the Christmas party.
2. No, she wasn't. / No, she was sad. / No, she wasn't. She was sad.
3. No, they weren't. / No, they were full. / No, they weren't. They were full.

[GRAM Writing]
1. The boy and his family **were in the living room**.
2. The Christmas tree **wasn't big**.
3. The boy **was excited** with the presents.
4. The girls **weren't happy** with the sweaters.

Unit 06. My Family Watched A Movie

[GRAM EXPRESSIONS] p.38
6-4-1-2-3-5

[GRAM CHECK UP] p.39
1. My family **visited** the museum yesterday.
2. We **played** badminton last Sunday.
3. We **cooked** pasta for dinner last night.
4. My family **watched** a movie last

Answers

weekend.

[GRAM PRACTICE] p.40

A.

1. i**nvite** friends
2. c**limb** a mountain
3. v**isit** a museum
4. e**njoy** the birthday party
5. **play** badminton
6. w**atch** a movie

B.

1. My sister **liked** her birthday presents.
2. We **didn't invite** our friends to the party.
3. My parents **planned** a trip to Paris.
4. I **didn't wait** for my brother at the station.
5. We **enjoyed** my brother's birthday.

[GRAM Comprehension] p.41

1. He planned **a surprise party for his mom**.
2. They prepared **many balloons**.
3. He invited **his mom's friends**.

[GRAM Speaking] p.42

1. It was great.
2. Yes, my family did. / Yes, my family enjoyed my birthday.
3. Yes, she did. / Yes, she cooked delicious food.
4. Yes, I did. / Yes, I invited my friends.

[GRAM Writing]

1. My family climbed a mountain last weekend.
2. My family enjoyed my birthday yesterday.
3. My family visited a museum last Saturday.

Unit 07. We Took A Trip

[GRAM EXPRESSIONS] p.44

3-6-5-2-1-4

[GRAM CHECK UP] p.45

1. We **bought** a big bag last week.
2. I **took** many pictures yesterday.
3. Sandy **didn't eat** seafood last night.
4. I **didn't swim** at the beach yesterday.

[GRAM PRACTICE] p.46

A.

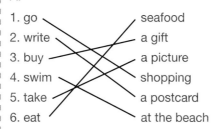

1. go — seafood
2. write — a gift
3. buy — a picture
4. swim — shopping
5. take — a postcard
6. eat — at the beach

B.

1. I **wrote** a postcard to Jason yesterday.
2. My sister swam at the beach last weekend.
3. We **didn't go** to the airport by bus.
4. Last winter we **took** many pictures in Guam.
5. I **didn't buy** gifts at the market.

[GRAM Comprehension] p.47

1. Yes, he did. / Yes, he went to San Diego.
2. He saw whales in the sea.
3. No, he didn't. / No, he bought some gifts. / No, he didn't. He bought some gifts.

[GRAM Speaking] p.48

didn't bring / left / the seat number

[GRAM Writing]

1. went, took
2. went, didn't bring
3. brought, said

Unit 08. Did You Have A Good Time?

[GRAM WORDS] p.50

5-1-3-6-2-4

[GRAM CHECK UP] p.51

1. did
2. didn't
3. didn't
4. did

[GRAM PRACTICE] p.52

1. museum
2. aquarium
3. fire station
4. amusement park
5. TV station

B.

1. Did you see
2. My class didn't go
3. What did you
4. When did you meet
5. Where did you go

[GRAM Comprehension] p. 53

1. Yes, she did.
2. She (especially) liked parrots.
3. No, she didn't. / No, she fed a horse. / No, she didn't. She fed a horse.

[GRAM Speaking] p. 54

A met
B took, went
C went, enjoyed
D ate
E watched, took
F had

[GRAM Writing]

When did you go
Did you have

What did you do

Did you see

Unit 09. I Am Making Cookies

[GRAM EXPRESSIONS] p.56

5-3-1-4-6-2

[GRAM PRACTICE] p.58

A.

1. cook, cooking
2. draw a picture, drawing a picture
3. play the piano, playing the piano
4. swim, swimming
5. take a photo, taking a photo

B.

1.

I am taking photos at the zoo.

I am not taking photos at the zoo.

2.

Nick is swimming in the river.

Nick is not swimming in the river.

3.

We are drawing pictures.

We are not drawing pictures.

[GRAM Comprehension] p.59

1. Yes, he is.
2. No, he isn't.
3. Yes, he is.

[GRAM Speaking] p.60

1. I am reading books.
2. I am reading The Ugly Duckling now.
3. I am going to the bookstore.
4. I am going with Sam.

[GRAM Writing]

1. The girl is collecting shells at the beach.
2. The girl is making a robot at home.
3. The girl is listening to music in her room.

Unit 10. I Was Doing My Homework

[GRAM WORDS] p.62

5-1-4-6-3-2

[GRAM CHECK UP] p.63

1. wasn't
2. weren't
3. was
4. were

[GRAM PRACTICE] p.64

A.

1. do h**omework**
2. l**earn** Taekwondo
3. take a w**alk**
4. r**ead** a book
5. take a piano l**esson**
6. r**ide** a bike

B.

1. was
2. were
3. weren't
4. was
5. were
6. weren't
7. wasn't
8. were

[GRAM Comprehension] p.65

1. No, she wasn't. / No, she wasn't. She was going to the library.
2. No, he wasn't. / No, he wasn't. He was going home.
3. Yes, he was.

[GRAM Speaking] p.66

A playing

B threw

C walking

D shouted

E listening

[GRAM Writing]

didn't watch

was learning

called

was taking

Unit 11. Are You Cleaning Your Room?

[GRAM EXPRESSIONS] p.68

5-3-1-6-2-4

[GRAM CHECK UP] p.69

1. **Is Jack setting** the table?
2. **Were you taking** out the trash?
3. **Was Jean watering** the plants?
4. **Are they washing** the dishes?

[GRAM PRACTICE] p.70

A.

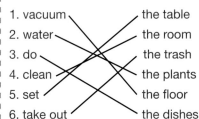

1. vacuum — the table
2. water — the room
3. do — the trash
4. clean — the plants
5. set — the floor
6. take out — the dishes

B.

1. **Is** Jason taking out the trash?
2. Were you **watering** the plants then?
3. **Are** you setting the table?
4. No, he **wasn't**.
5. **Were** you vacuuming the floor?

[GRAM Comprehension] p.71

1. No, she wasn't. She was washing the dishes.
2. Yes, he was.
3. No, he wasn't. He was cooking dinner for his family.

[GRAM Speaking] p.72

1. No, she isn't. She is watering the plants.

2. No, he wasn't. He was cleaning his room.
3. She is doing the dishes.

[GRAM Writing] p.72
1. The man is **vacuuming the floor**.
2. The woman is **watering the plants**.
3. The boy is **taking out the trash**.
4. The girl is **washing the dishes**.

Unit 12. What Was He Doing?

[GRAM EXPRESSIONS] p.74
6-2-5-3-4-1

[GRAM CHECK UP] p.75
1. playing
2. singing
3. writing
4. practicing

[GRAM PRACTICE] p.76
A.
1. interview
2. sing in the chorus
3. see the stars
4. play music
5. exercise
6. watch a movie

B.
1. What
2. Where
3. What
4. What
5. Where

[GRAM Comprehension] p.77
A.
1. She was holding a large box.
2. She was going to her club.
3. Yes, he was.

[GRAM Speaking] p.78
1. Where were you going?

2. What were you doing there?
3. Who were in the library?
4. What were they doing?

[GRAM Writing]
1. Where was she going?
2. Who was she talking with?
3. What were the students doing?

Unit 13. It Is Under The Desk

[GRAM EXPRESSIONS] p.80
4-5-3-1-2

[GRAM CHECK UP] p.81
1. The doll is **on** the desk.
2. The cat is **under** the piano.
3. The chairs are **in front of** the bed.
4. The hats are **in** the box.
5. The window is **behind** the desk.
6. The English book is **under** the chair.

[GRAM PRACTICE] p.82
A.
1. map, wall
2. hat, bed
3. doll, bookshelf
4. box, closet
5. backpack, floor
6. TV, window

B.
1. under → in
   The shirt is in the closet.
2. behind → in front of
   The TV is in front of the window.
3. in → on
   The cups are on the bookshelf.
4. on → under
   The backpack is under the chair.
5. on → in front of
   The desks are in front of the window.

[GRAM Comprehension] p.83
1. It is on the desk.
2. No, they aren't. / No, they aren't next to the bookshelves.
3. They are under the bed.

[GRAM Speaking] p.84
1. Yes, I have a big window in my room.
2. It is in front of the window.
3. It is next to the desk.
4. It is on the desk.

[GRAM Writing]
(1) in front of the window
(2) on the desk
(3) under the bed
(4) on the wall

Unit 14. It Is Next To The Hospital

[GRAM WORDS] p.86
2-5-4-6-1-3

[GRAM CHECK UP] p.87
1. The bank is **next to** the hospital.
2. The police station is **across from** the park.
3. The hospital is **between** the park and the post office.
4. The fire station is **next to** the police station.

[GRAM PRACTICE] p.88
A.
1. post office
2. bank
3. hospital
4. police station
5. fire station
6. movie theater

B.
1. movie theater
2. post office
3. bank
4. police station

[GRAM Comprehension] p.89
1. It is next to the school.
2. It is across from the school.
3. It is between the Grace Park and the post office.

[GRAM Speaking] p.90
1. No, it is across from the library.
2. It is between the bank and the restaurant.
3. No, it is next to the police station.

[GRAM Writing]
1. The library is **next to the post office**.
2. The restaurant is **between the bank and the movie theater**.
3. The park is **across from the hospital**.

Unit 15. There Is A Zoo In My Town

[GRAM EXPRESSIONS] p.92
2-4-3-6-1-5

[GRAM CHECK UP] p.93
1. is
2. are
3. are
4. is

[GRAM PRACTICE] p.94
A.
1. concert hall
2. train station
3. fish market
4. old palace
5. library

B.
1. There isn't a concert hall
2. There aren't old palaces
3. Is there a library
4. There is a museum
5. Are there many people

[GRAM Comprehension] p.95
1. Yes, there are. / Yes, there are. There are special reading programs for children.
2. Yes, there is. / Yes, there is. There is a small movie theater for children.
3. No, there isn't. / No, there isn't. There is a beautiful garden in front of the library.

[GRAM Speaking] p.96
(A) There **are** two interesting places in my town.
(B) There **is** a famous fish market in my town.
(E) There **are** many big trees in the palace.
(D) There **is** an old palace in my town, too.
(C) There **are** many people in the market every day.

[GRAM Writing]
(1) is a large painting
(2) is a woman
(3) are two boys
(4) are a man and a girl

Unit 16 Where Is The Bakery?

[GRAM EXPRESSIONS] p.98
3-6-5-1-4-2

[GRAM CHECK UP] p.99
1. right
2. straight, left
3. straight, right
4. corner

[GRAM PRACTICE] p.100
A.
1. ice cream shop
2. stationery store
3. bakery
4. bookstore
5. supermarket

B.
1. next to
2. at the corner
3. across from
4. turn left
5. turn right

[GRAM Comprehension] p.101
1. It is next to the stationery store.
2. It is at the corner.
3. Go straight on block. Turn left at the corner and go straight.

[GRAM Speaking] p.102
An ice cream shop is **next to** the bookstore.
Go straight and turn right **at the corner**.

[GRAM Writing]
1. notebook
2. stationery store
3. next to, turn left

Index

amusement park

aquarium

ask to pass the salt

bakery

bank

be late

be noisy

be on time

be quiet

behind the desk

bookstore

buy a gift

cheat

Children's Day

Christmas

clean the room

climb

clothing store

collect shells

concert hall

cook

cover one's mouth

do homework

do the dishes

draw a picture

eat seafood

enjoy

exercise

fight

fire station

fish market

give up one's seat

go shopping

Halloween

hospital

ice cream shop

in front of the computer

in the closet

interview

invite

learn Taekwondo

library

litter

movie theater

museum

New Year's Day

old palace

on the wall

play badminton

play baseball

play basketball

play computer games

play music

play soccer

play tennis

play the piano

play volleyball

police station

post office

read a book

ride a bike

run

see the stars

set the table

sing in the chorus

stationery store

supermarket

swim

swim at the beach

take a photo

take a piano lesson

take a picture

take a walk

take off shoes

take out the trash

Thanksgiving

train station

TV station

under the chair

vacuum the floor

Valentine's Day

visit

wait one's turn

watch

watch a movie

water the plants

wear a helmet

wear knee pads

write a postcard

GramGram Plus 3

First Printing 2014.3.20

Author Hyunjeong, Kim

Consultant Prof. Eunyoung, Park

Editorial Supervisor LLS English Research Center

Publisher Kiseon, Lee

Publishing Company JPLUS

62, World Cup-ro 31-gil, Mapo-gu, Seoul, Korea

Telephone 02-332-8320

Fax 02-332-8321

Homepage www.jplus114.com

Registration Number 10-1680

Registration Date 1998.12.09

ISBN 979-11-5601-017-3(64740)

ⓒ JPLUS 2014

memo

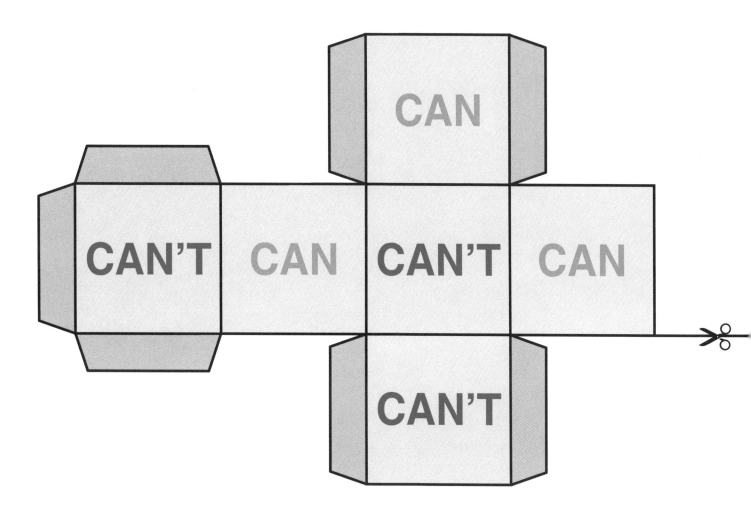

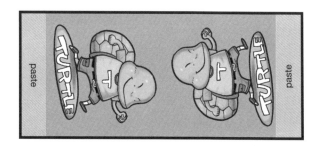

You _____ make fun of your classmates.

6

You _____ be late.

7

Cover

School Rules

You _____ fight with classmates.

5

You _____ cheat.

You _____ in the hallway.

4

You _____ be quiet in class.

2

You _____ litter.

3

Unit 04 Spinner p.31

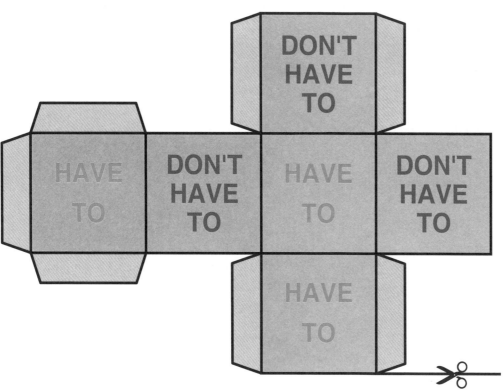

Unit 11 Coin Flick Game p.73

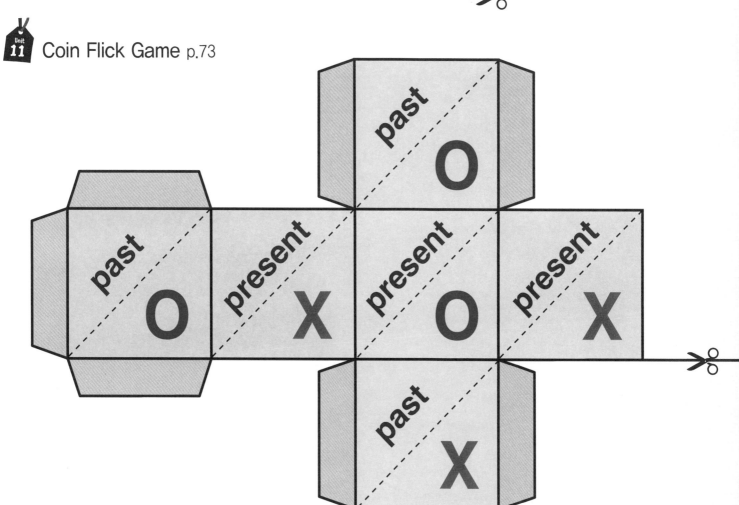

Unit
07 Memory Game p.49

ride a bike   cook   take a photo   play the piano

draw a picture   read a book   write a story   swim

watch a movie   collect shells   play the guitar   play basketball

play the violin   play baseball   listen to music   make a robot

SHE	**HE**	**THEY**
HE	**THEY**	**SHE**
YOU	**SHE**	**THEY**
play music	interview	see the stars
watch movies	sing in the chorus	exercise
act	read books	cook

 In My Room p.13

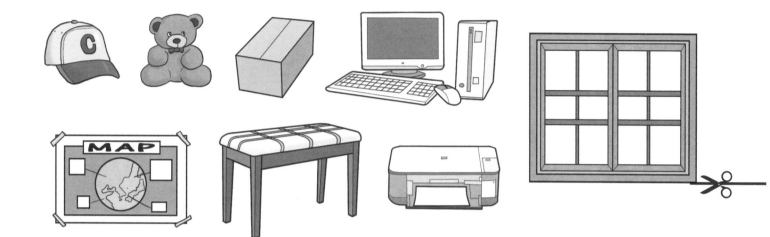

 Where Is It? p.91

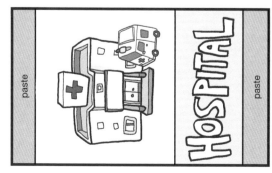